IMO Workbook Class III

CBSE ICSE State Boards Olympiads   NTSE

School Level Entrance Examinations

Mathematics Leve I and Level II for Grade III

CBSE, IGCSE, State Bards and Olympiads

Chandan Sukumar Sengupta

Creative Learning Series

IMO Workbook Class III

CBSE ICSE   State Boards   Olympiads   NTSE School Level Entrance Examinations
Chandan Sukumar Sengupta

ISBN   : 9798889510130

There are mathematical problems which require knowledge of more than one thematic areas. Such problems are incorporated in the collections of Composite worksheets. In this workbook such composite worksheets are more in number. For all students it would be better if they acquire such skills in advance before moving through the composite worksheets.

Other books in this series are as follows:
1. Handbook of Mathematics
2. Creative Mathematics Book 7 Part 1
3. Olympiad and Talent
4. Aspirations of Mathematics
5. My Own Book of School Mathematics.

All these books are suitable for students of School stage having age group 11 to 13 years.

This Workbook is meant primarily for students of Standard V. Other aspirants having affinity of revising their skills and competence of that level can take it as their source book.

This workbook is prepared for students of Class III

Contents

CONTENTS

Preface

We learn many things and also come across many experiences in our daily life. Some of such experiences strike our mind to a greater extent and some of the gained experiences remain as an off-sided thing because of the ignorance of our mind.

Learning, as one can go through in life, is not any forceful effort of the mind. It should have a support of mind, body and intellect. Then only it can bring variations in our thought process. There are so many faculties through which the learning of a student might move on. It may be a hybrid faculty combining some of the inter-related streams of study; such as Astronomy and Physics will jointly make the faculty of Astro-Physics; Geology and Information Technology will make the faculty of Geo-Informatics and many more.

Parents often claim that their ward is proficient in some of the selected faculties and work with limitations in some other. Actually the trend of the study of a learner is a non-identifiable trend because of the chance of its alterations in relation to time. One cannot guess about the affinity of the brain before the age of 13 of a student. Learning affinity and allied success largely depends upon the combination of parenting and related service linings. Only parenting and any service lining without parenting may not bring any desired result in time. Combination of both the factor can link up the milestones leading ultimately towards success.

India Government has decided to centralise the process of admissions to various Graduate level Medical Colleges. This admission process will be accomplished by the entrance examinations taken up by National Testing Agency (or NTA). Aspirants having a willingness to attain the Entrance Examination conducted by NTA or other such testing agency should have access to the knowledge system duly prescribed for the prevalent knowledge drilling and information delivery pattern. Preparation for such kind of testing is also a job which requires prolonged involvement of the fellow learner. The learner with such willingness should have a strong base of knowledge which will ensure the smooth and swift propagation of mind and intellect through the definite path of success.

We restrict our discussion to the limit of the content areas for which the present workbook is having some inputs. Students of class six should have a proper understanding of basic shapes, number system, daily life problems and ecological concerns. Most of the problems are related to daily experiences and normal operational concerns.

It is expected that students should go on facing day to day problems from science, mathematics and humanities. They should also address problems related to high order thinking skills. They also participate in online digital classes and social media platforms for exploring relevant information on certain topic. Hunting merely for information may not fulfil the purpose in particular. Information duly collected should have adequate alignment with facts and figures for ensuring the process of remembering and recollecting such kinds of learning during need.

We are also incorporating few words from the faculty of mathematics. Most of the part of publication is based on the pattern of questions people select for Olympiads, Talent Search Examinations and other competitive examinations of similar nature. This publication also introduces a learner with some apprehensions of Critical thinking.

Mathematics deals with some fundamental aspects related to time and space. We all learn different rules and related operations starting from our elementary stage of schooling. Different students take the subject differently as per their interest and willingness. Some students calculate values with adequate speed and some other students do the same with lot of difficulties. We also point out the development of fear related to Mathematics in the mind of some of the fellow students. We cannot analyse the possible reasons of the development of such fear in the mind of students. This development cannot be generalised. It is not developed in the minds of all the fellow students. Things often become difficult when our fellow ward fail to correlate the linkages of real life problems with that of mathematical ones. It is the main reason of the lack of proper orientation in the process of the development of mathematical skills. A skilful student can correlate both the aspects of mathematics and real life problems with much efficiency. A skilful student of mathematics should be a good observer, a perfect planner, optimum analyser and abled calculator. Some students can take much time in solving any individual mathematical problem that compared to the time taken by the other fellow from the same peer group. This book is designed to expose a student to different types of mathematical problems from the allied fields of the curriculum specified for the middle school. It is expected that this workbook can equip a student in different ways and enable them to acquire mathematical skills with a long lasting impression in mind.

The Curriculum

The curriculum recommended by CBSE and ICSE are on the same format like those developed and implemented by different state level educational organisations. After integrating all such streams a common core of the curriculum is duly obtained for making the book a widely applicable one. Some of the mathematical problems are from past test papers. In some papers there may remain some questions of identical format. All such questions will be addressed only after proper understanding of the relevant theories.

Some of inter related areas are converged to bring compactness in the representation of the content areas. There may exist some types of questions in more than two places with an aspiration of exhibiting its composite nature.

Before moving through the collection of worksheets and related fields of activities it is recommended for all the students that one should go through the content areas duly provided by the authority of examinations.

After such thorough practices one can opt for the composite worksheets with some easiness.

Major areas of the curriculum are as follows:
1. The number system and its application in our day to day life.
2. Representing a whole number in the number line.
3. Factors and multiples.
4. Measurements of length, mass temperature and time.
5. Basic shapes of two dimensions and three dimensions.
6. Mean, median and mode.

Numbers may be divisible by 2 (Even Numbers) or may not be divisible by 2 (Odd Numbers). Numbers having only 2 factors ; 1 and the number itself are called prime numbers.

A list of prime numbers between 1 and 200 :

2, 3, 5, 7, 11, 13, 17, 19, 23, 29, 31, 37, 41, 43, 47, 53, 59, 61, 67, 71, 73, 79, 83, 89, 97, 101, 103, 107, 109, 113, 127, 131, 137, 139, 149, 151, 157, 163, 167, 173, 179, 181, 191, 193, 197, and 199.

2 and 3 are a pair of consecutive prime numbers.

A prime number 2 less or 2 more than another prime are called twin prime numbers. You can find more than a pair of twin primes from the list of primes provided.

For example: 11 and 13; 17 and 19; 29 and 31; and so on..

Points to Remember

We can draw only one line passing through two given points but uncountable number of lines can be drawn passing through a point. Lines, rays and line segments are called one dimensional figure. They have only measurable lengths. Lengths of lines and rays are not finite. We can trace out only one line segment passing through three collinear points. We can draw three lines by using any two out of three non-collinear points. There may be several line segments lying on the same line. Many lines can be drawn passing through a definite point. Only one line can be drawn passing through two or three given points. Two concurrent lines , a pair of concurrent line segments and concurrent rays always lie on a single plane.

Triangle is a smallest polygon having three vertices, three angles and three sides. Properties of triangles are widely discussed in the field of studies related to geometry. Here we discuss the properties of triangle related to interior angles, exterior angles, relationship of sides and relationship of other sub-ordinate parts.

It is easy to establish correlations between angles, sides and vertices of a triangle. This shape also provides a basic platform for the study of properties of other polygons. Those aspects can be discussed in outline.

We can draw a triangle by using three non collinear points located on a single plane. Lines joining any two of the three non collinear points can form a closed figure having three sides, three vertices and three angles. Such a polygon is the figure we are discussing about. If two adjacent triangles share a common arm then the resultant closed figure will be a quadrilateral. In this way triangles can be located in polygons having more than three sides.

Triangles are classified on the basis of their sides and angles. Isosceles right triangle and scalene right triangle can be drawn. Construction of equilateral right triangle is not possible. There are some other combination in triangles which is not possible in actual construct. Some of such examples of absurdity are as follows:

1. Triangles having two obtuse angles or two right angles.
2. Triangle having interior angles more than or less than two right angles.
3. Triangle having two exterior angle as right angle.
4. Two congruent triangles having three corresponding angles equal to each other and three corresponding sides unequal to each other.

While constructing a triangle it I observed that third side of any triangle will be, either greater than the difference of the length of other two sides, or less than the sum total of other two sides.

Triangles are the smallest possible closed figure formed by joining three straight lines. Other polygons, such as quadrilaterals, pentagons, hexagons can be obtained by joining triangles side by side.

Four sided closed figures are called quadrilaterals. Rectangles, squares, trapezoids, kites are all examples of quadrilaterals.

Sum total of all the interior angles of a quadrilateral is equal to four right angles.

A quadrilateral having any one angle as reflex angle is called a concave quadrilateral. On the other hand quadrilaterals having angles less than a straight angle are convex quadrilaterals.

Rectangle is a type of quadrilateral having opposite sides equal to each other and parallel to each other. All the interior angles of a rectangle are right angles. On the basis of such property we can say that square is a special type of rectangle having length and breadth equal to each other.

Parallelogram is a type of quadrilateral in which opposite sides are equal to each other and parallel to each other, but none of the interior angles are right angles. Rhombus is a special type of parallelogram having length and breadth equal to each other.

A process of measurement is used in mathematics is often called the decimal process. Decimal stands for the number of digits used to represent any number. Ten stands for decim; that is why numbers represented by using digits 9,8,7,6,5,4,3,2,1 and 0 are called decimal numbers. Measurements of lengths, mass and time are called scalar units. Other big units are formed on the basis of decimal relations. All the metric measurements are related through the multiples of 10. 10 mm length , for example is equal to 1 cm; 10 cm = 1 dm and 10 dm = 1 m. that means 100 cm can be represented as 1 m.

A linear scale represents both cm marking and inches marking. A foot rule has markings of 12 inches on one side and 30 cm on the other.

A Factor tree represents a comsite number along with constituent factors.

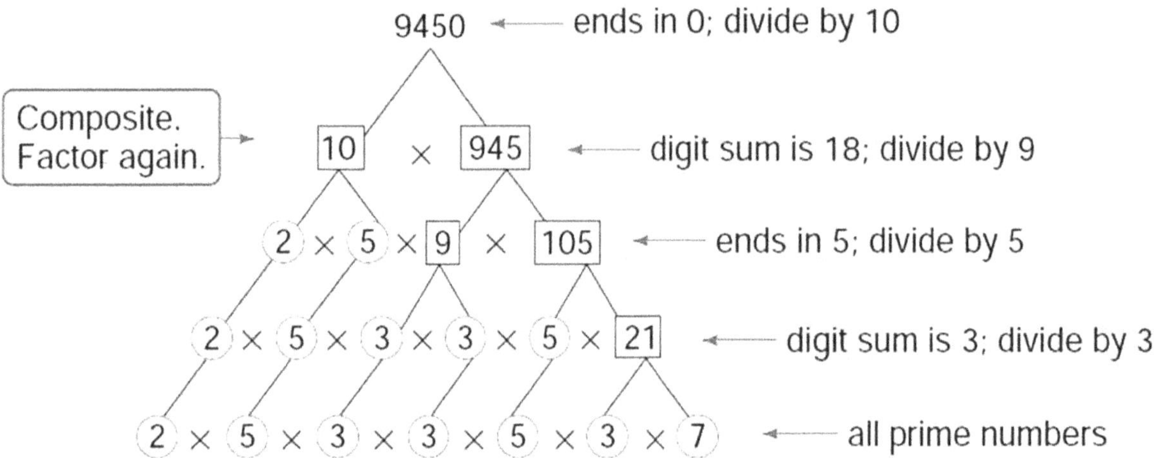

So, the prime factorization of 9450 is $2 \times 3^3 \times 5^2 \times 7$.

All prime numbers have only two factors: 1 and the number itself.

To calculate area of a rectangle we can multiply length and breadth.

$$A = s^2$$

$$A = 3 \times 3$$

$$A = 9 \text{ m}^2$$

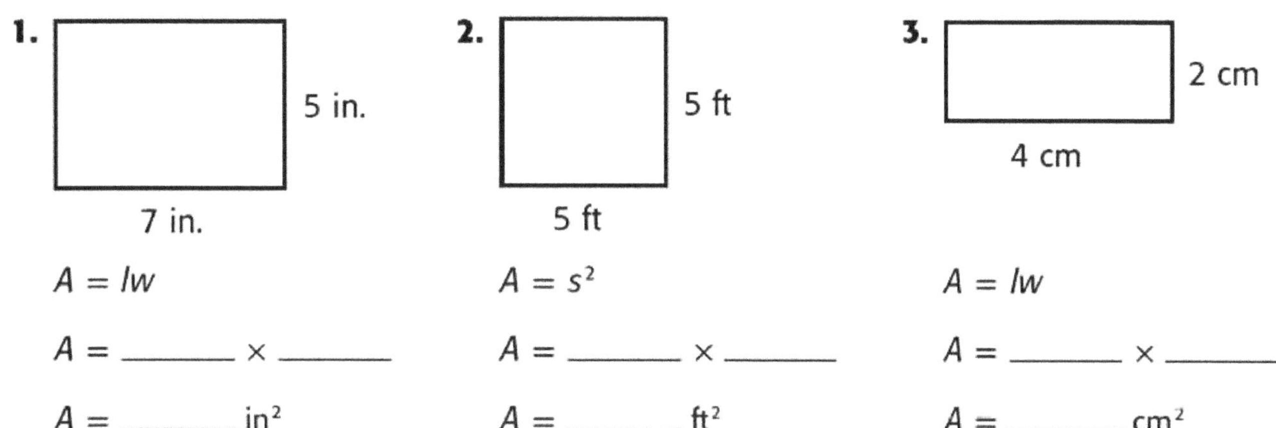

1.

$A = lw$

$A = \underline{\hspace{2cm}} \times \underline{\hspace{2cm}}$

$A = \underline{\hspace{2cm}} \text{ in}^2$

2.

$A = s^2$

$A = \underline{\hspace{2cm}} \times \underline{\hspace{2cm}}$

$A = \underline{\hspace{2cm}} \text{ ft}^2$

3.

$A = lw$

$A = \underline{\hspace{2cm}} \times \underline{\hspace{2cm}}$

$A = \underline{\hspace{2cm}} \text{ cm}^2$

A bar graph is used to compare categories of data. The categories are written on the horizontal axis. The scale, which is separated into equal parts or intervals, is written on the vertical axis. A line graph is used to show how a data set changes over a period of time. Generally the time interval is shown on the horizontal axis. The scale is written on the vertical axis.

1. Revision Works

Revision 1

1: A train is running at an average speed of 80 km per hour. It is covering up 4 km 4 m more in every interval of 10 minutes than that of a car. Find the average speed of the car.

2. Observe following statements:

I: 2 is an even prime number.

II: 2 has no factors other than 1 and the number itself.

III: 2 has another factor which is also a factor of all the other natural numbers.

IV: All the other even numbers are multiples of 2.

Select which of the statements mentioned above are true.

A: Only I   B: Only II   C: Only I and III   D: All

3. 3. Some of the statements regarding prime and composite numbers are given below.

I : 1 is not a prime or composite number.

II : Two is the only even prime number.

III: All odd numbers are not prime.

IV: All composite numbers can be written as product of prime numbers.

V: 101 has only two factors 1 and the number itself. That is why it is a prime number

Which of the above statements are true?

A: Only I   B: All   C: I, II and III   D: Only II, III and IV

4. How many digits will be there in product of 1001 and 999?

5. $11/13^{\text{th}}$ of a natural number is equal to 13,26,039. The number is …………..

6. Complete the following statements:

    a) The number 365 is divisible by both __________ and __________.

    b) The number 121 has two factors other than 1. Those two factors are ______ and __________.

    c) Product of two numbers is 284. Their HCF is 132 and LCM is __________.

    d) There are ______ diagonals in a hexagon.

    e) We can subtract _____ and _____ from 134,000 and 129,000,000 respectively to make them exactly divisible by 11.

7. In forming numbers from given digits, we should be careful to see if the conditions under which the numbers are to be formed are satisfied. Thus, to form the greatest four digit number from 7, 8, 3, 5 without repeating a single digit, we need to use all four digits, the greatest number can have only 8 as the leftmost digit.

8. A three digit greatest number is divisible by both 3 and 6. This number is also divisible by __________. This number must be an ________________ number.

9. The cost of petrol is `60 per litre. A petrol bunk sells 750 litres of petrol on a day. How much money do they get at the end of the day?

10. You live in Ahmedabad and you travelled 400 m by bus to reach the nearest station. Then you take a train to reach Gandhi Nagar which is 15 km. away. Then you take a cab to reach your aunt's house which is 18 km. away.

    i. How much distance did you travel to reach your aunt's house?

    ii. If you travel for 7 days like this how much distance would you travel?

11. Interior angle of a regular polygon varies on the basis of number of sides. Sum total of all the exterior angles is equal to 360^0. Measure of the exterior angle of a regular polygon is 120^0. That is why magnitude of interior angle is 60^0 as both exterior and interior angles supplement each other.

Revision 2

Square is a special type of rectangle having length and breadth equal to each other. All the interior angles in both the cases are right angles.

1: Identify solid shapes formed by using following nets.

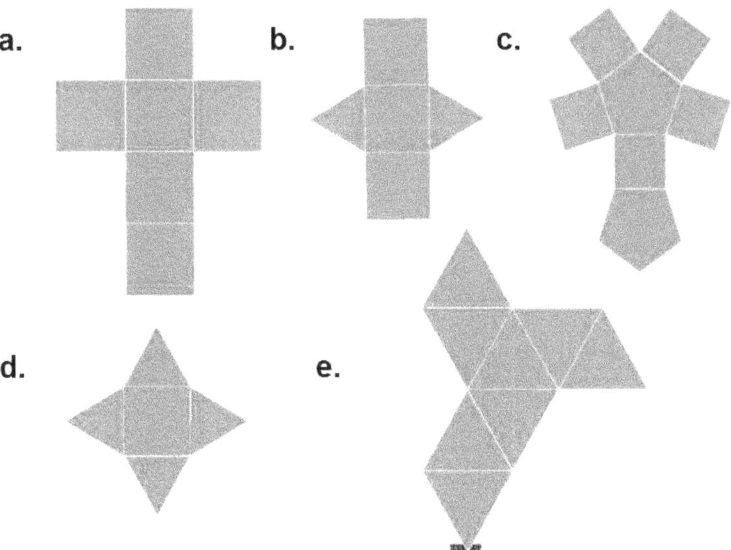

2. Puma formed six digit greatest and five digit smallest number by using different digits. None of digits were repeated while forming each of the numbers. Find out sum total of both the digits.

3. Somerfield observed that a train is taking 1 m 12 s to cross a light post. What is the length of that train? Consider average speed of that train 18 km/h.

4. $1/11^{th}$ of 11,022 + $1/13^{th}$ of 13,026 + $1/15^{th}$ of 15,030 = ……………

5. Find out unknown angles.

a.

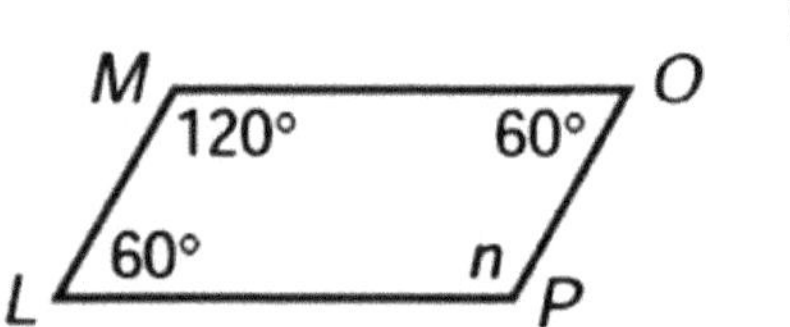

b.

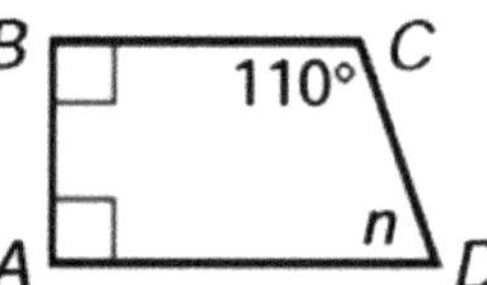

c.

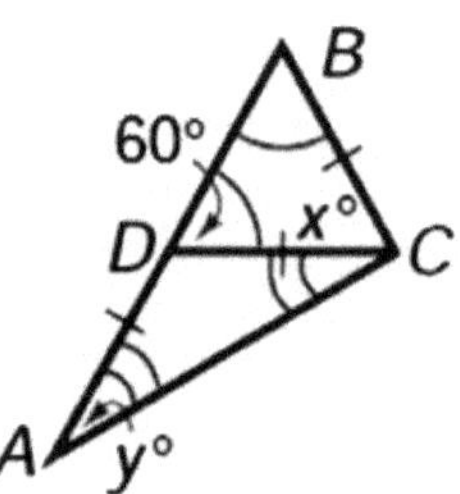

d.

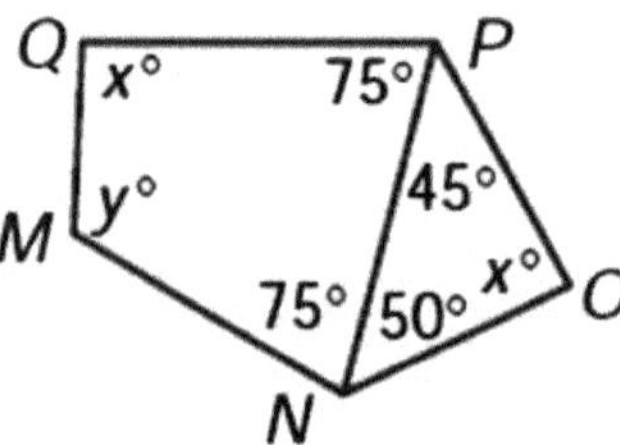

e.

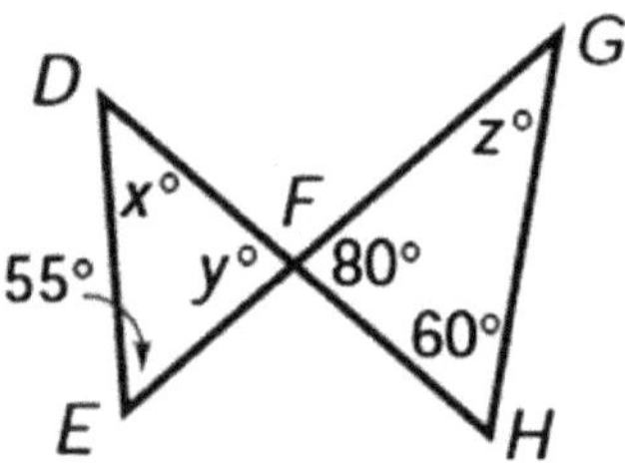

f.

6. Four angles of a quadrilateral are in the ratio of $1: 2: 3: 4$. Find out the greatest angle.

7. 12% of $\dfrac{1100}{144} + 13\%$ of $\dfrac{1200}{169} = $ …………..

8. Veena rides her bike to the park for 18 minutes at an average speed of 9 m per second to meet a friend. Veena arrives at the park at 11:00 a.m. and stays there for 58 minutes. Her friend will arrive there at 12:15 p.m. they had a meeting for 32 minutes.
Try to answer the following questions.
A. What is the distance between the park and Veena's house?
B. How long could Veena have to wait for her friend?
C. How long does Veena stay at the park?   D. When will Veena leave to go home?

9. There are some similarities between a parallelogram and a rhombus.
I: None of the interior angles are right angles.
II: Opposite sided are parallel to each other.
III: Opposite sides are equal to each other.
IV: Sum total of interior angles of each polygon is 3600
Which of the statements are not true?
A: Only I, II and III   B: Only I   C: All   D: None

10. Similarities between a parallelogram and a rhombus. Strike out the wrong one.
I: None of the interior angles are right angles.
II: Opposite sided are parallel to each other.
III: Opposite sides are equal to each other.
IV: Sum total of interior angles of each polygon is 3600

11. Two graphs display members of different clubs and dance practice performed by Nikita per day for five consecutive days.

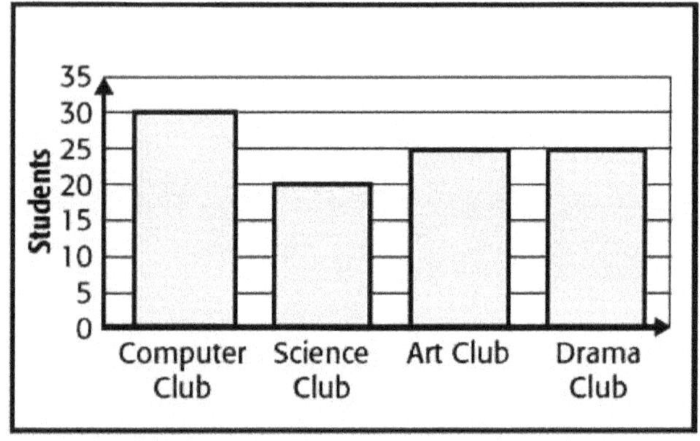

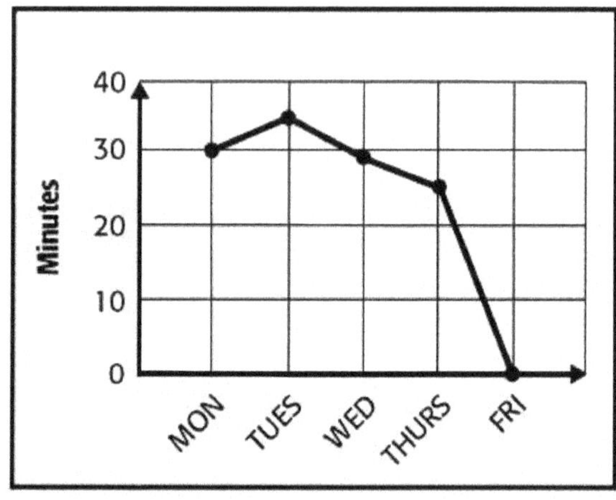

Graph 1: Club Members   Graph 2: Dance Practice

A: Students joining science club also joined computer club. How many additional students are there in computer club?

B. The interval f time in Grah 2 is …………

C: ………………………… is the most polular club and ……………… is least popular.

12. A circle of diameter 280 cm is exactly fitted concentrically inside another circle of diameter 2.8 m for obtaining a design find the area enclosed by linings of both the circle.

13. 11th multiple of 8,000 and 8th multiple of 11,000 added to obtain a value which is _____________ more than the smallest 6 digit number.

14. How many five digit numbers are there in all?

2. Test Paper II

1: Which solid shapes will be formed by using each of the following nets?

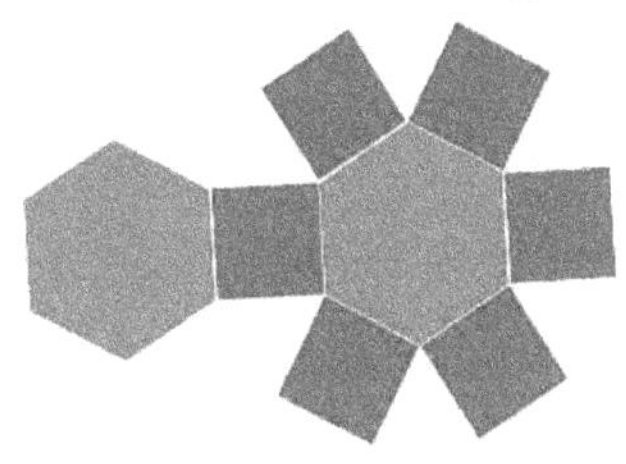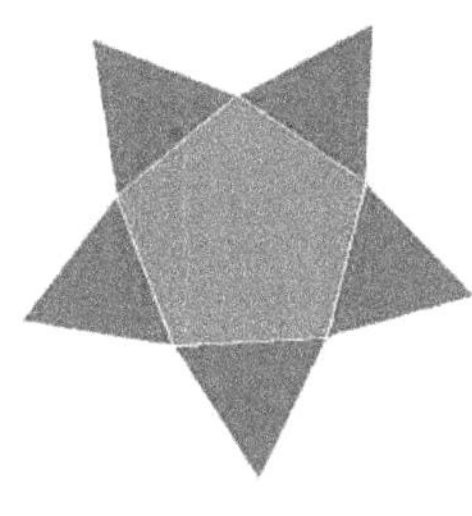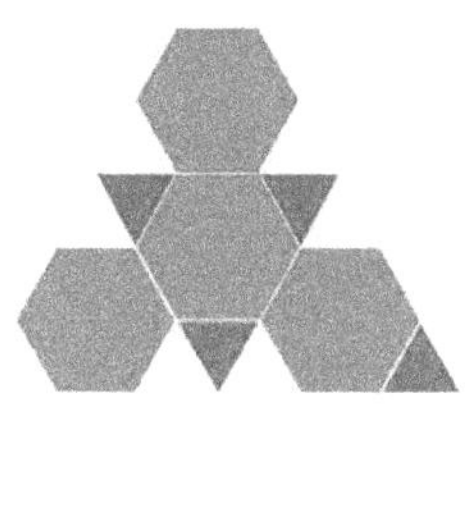

A   B   C

2. Solve the following

a. $-3r + 10 = 15r - 8$ b. $7 + 3x - 12x = 3x + 1$

c. $w - 2 + 2w = 6 + 5w$ d. $10(g + 5) = 2(g + 9)$

e. $-9(t - 2) = 4(t - 15)$ f. $(3x + 9) = -2(2x + 6)$

g. $\left(\dfrac{19a}{25} + \dfrac{121}{125} a + \dfrac{139}{250} a + \dfrac{7}{8} a \right) \left(1 + \dfrac{1}{1000} \right) X \dfrac{1}{1001} = 12.125$

h. $(1 + x + x^2) = \dfrac{27}{1-x}$; Calculate $(x^3 - 12 x^2 + 11 x)$

3. Product of three consecutive number is equal to 720. Find out the numbers.

4. 4% of 5% of a natural number is equal to $\dfrac{121}{500}$. Find out sixth multiple of that number.

5. Three angles of a quadrilateral are in the ratio of 3: 5: 7. Is it possible to work out magnitude of the fourth angle? If yes, work out probable magnitude of the fourth angle.

6. 21st multiple of a number exceeds 42nd multiple smallest five digit number by 1050. Find out the number.

7. What least number should be subtracted from greatest five digit number to make it divisible by 4?

8. Calculate shaded portions by using fractions.

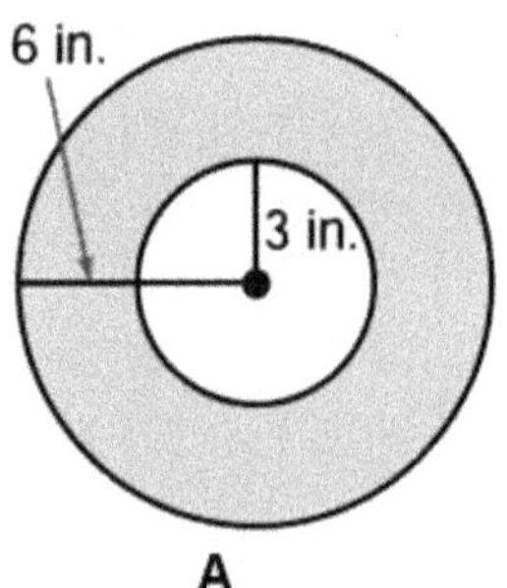

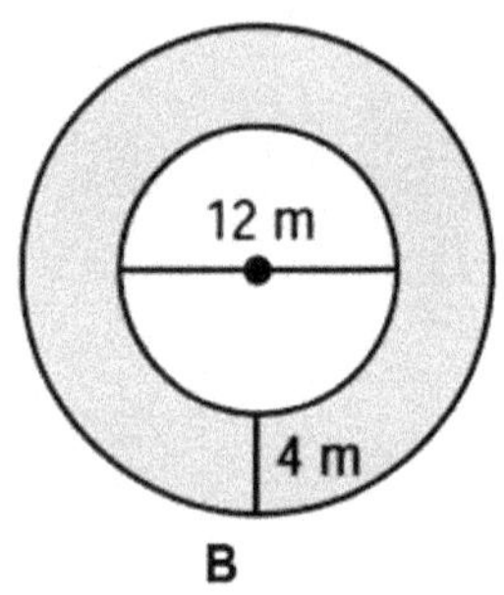

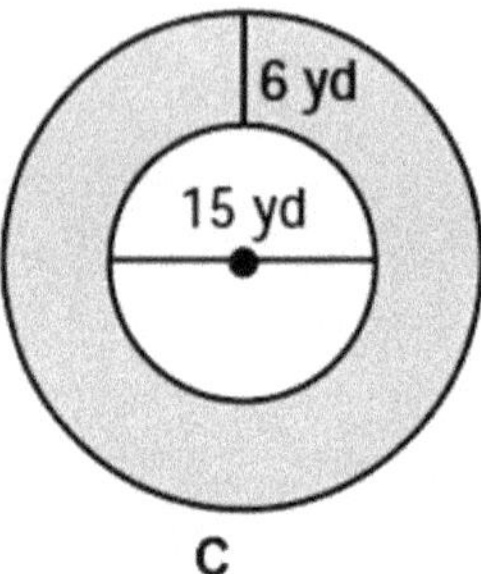

9. How many cubical bricks each of side 16 cm will be used to construct a wall of dimension 6 m 40 cm, 4 m and 32 cm?

10. Increase of $36\ ^0$ C is recorded in a city during day time. Calculate corresponding increase in ^{0} F.

11. 20% of a number is 640 more than fourth multiple of six digit smallest number. Find out the number.

12. Write in standard form:

$$125 + \frac{121}{125} + \frac{345}{625} + \frac{39}{40} + \frac{21}{25} + \frac{1001}{1000} + \frac{321}{400} - 121.324$$

13. Neha reached her school 5 minutes earlier than scheduled time. Her wrist watch was displaying 100: 45 a.m. The watch was running late by 9 minutes. Normal schedule of assembly is ....

14. A square of side 20 cm is exactly fitted uniformly inside another square of side 30 cm for obtaining a design. Find the area enclosed by linings of both the squares.

***

3. Test Paper III

1: The heights of six mountains are 8200 m, 6000 m, 8600 m, 7500 m, 8800 m and 6500 m . Based on this information, What is the approximate average height of the mountains?

2. CE is the angle bisector and Triangle displayed in diagram is an isosceles triangle. Find out all the interior angles of the triangle.

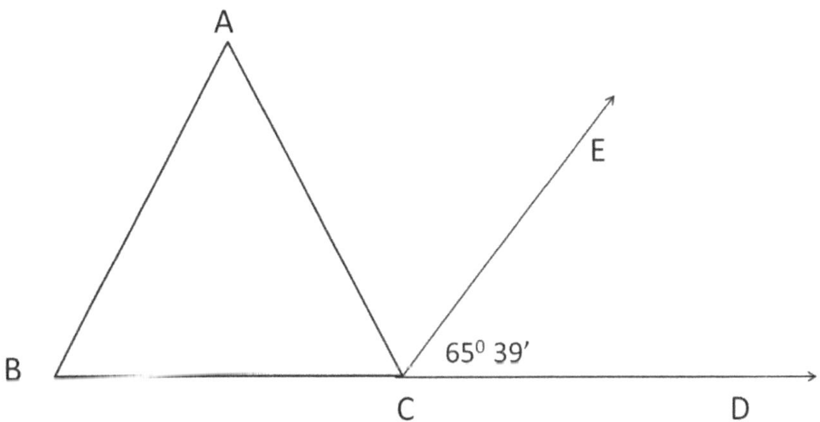

3. $(1 + x + 2x + \ldots 10{,}000x)(3x - 4) = 0$; then find out simplest value of $(9x + \dfrac{936}{1440} x + \dfrac{21}{16} x)$

4. The heights of 10 students, measured in cm are as follows:

143, 132, 150, 139, 128, 135, 151, 146, 141, 149

A: What is the height of the shortest girl?

B: If another student of height 139 cm is included in the group then average height of students will be changed by ……. Cm.

5. What fraction of all the natural numbers starting from 1 to 50 are prime numbers?

6. Write in standard form: $\left(\frac{121}{100} + \frac{121}{1000} + \frac{121}{10000} + \frac{121}{10} + 121\right)$

7. Work out unknown angles.

a.

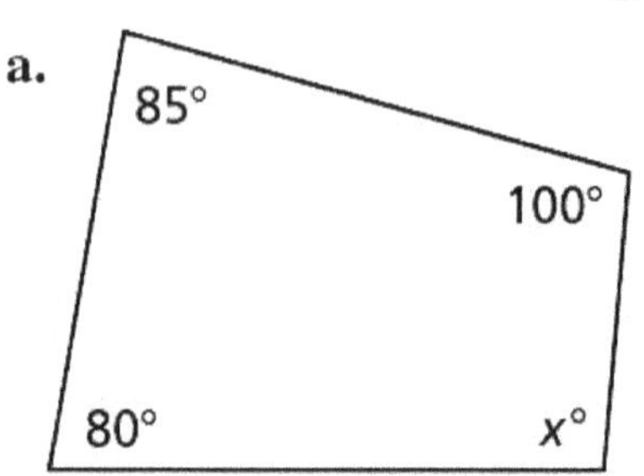

b.

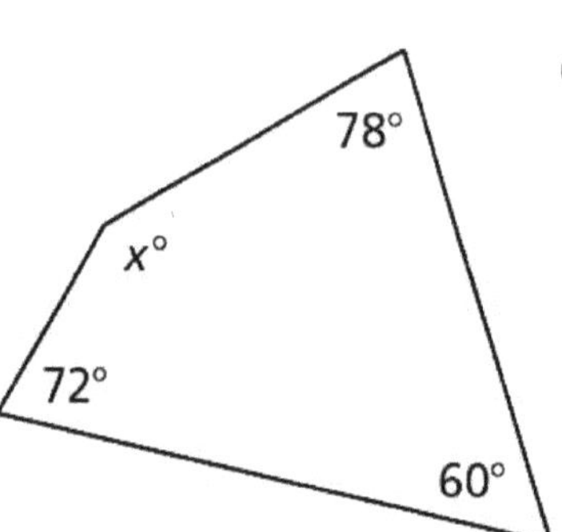

c.

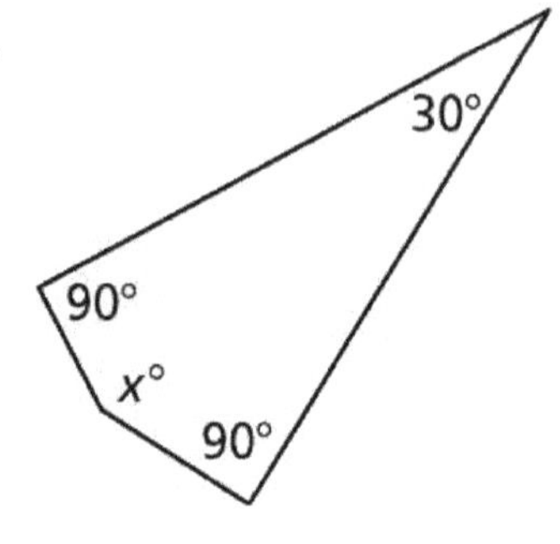

8. Calculate area of shaded portions.

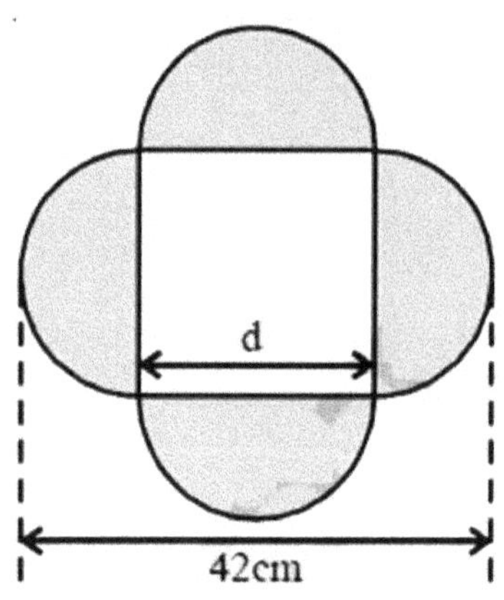

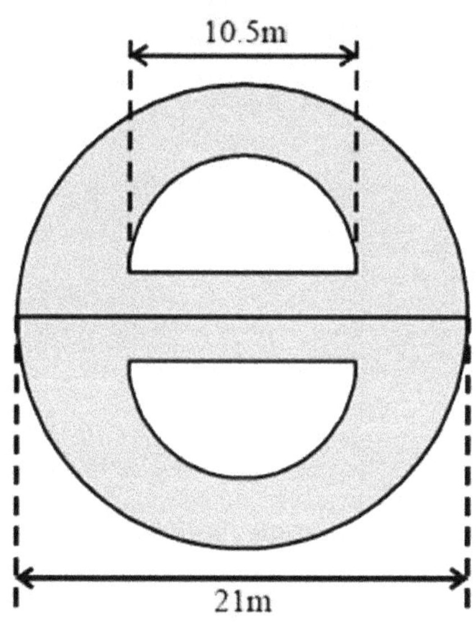

9. If following pattern continues then total number of cubes required for 16th step will be

....

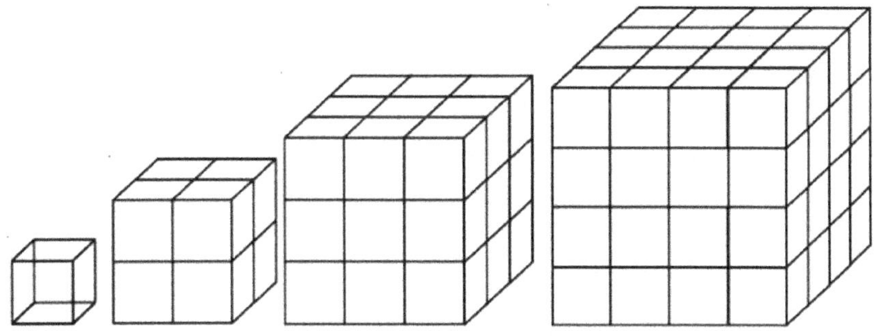

10. Cost of sugar is increased by 20%. A family wants to keep monthly expenditure on sugar unchanged. Consumption of sugar to be curtailed by that family in percentage will be …………

11: Arrange the following shapes as per their increasing number of faces.

Cylinder, Sphere, Cuboid, Triangular Prism, Rectangular Pyramid.

12. A train is running at an average speed of 80 km per hour. It is covering up 4 km 4 m more in every interval of 10 minutes than that of a car. Find the average speed of the car.

13. A half filled oil container is used to store residue oil of capacity 125 liters. After filling the residue three eighth of the container remained empty. Find the capacity of the container.

14. One tenth of a container is equal to 16 cans of capacity 8 liters each. The entire container can hold ___________ liters of oil.

15. What least number must be subtracted from 219.376 to make the result exactly divisible by 219?   [Ans: 0.157]

16. A train, moving at the speed of 15 m per second, is taking 20 seconds to cross a telephone post. This train can take ________ seconds to cross a 1.5 km long platform. [Ans : 2 minutes]

17. Roshanlal can finish a work in 16 days while working 5 hours a day. He can finish the same work in ……….. days while working 4 hours a day.

18. Rani is buying light bulbs for her Christmas decorations. She buys 1020 but when she gets to the cash, she has to put back 3 hundred 13 because they are broken. How many light bulbs does Marie buy?

19. There are two combinations of packs containing pens and pencils. Packet one containing 6 pens and 5 pencils costs Rs 128. Packet B containing 5 pens and 6 pencils costs Rs 103. Calculate the cost of a new pack containing 10 pens and 10 pencils of such type?

A: Rs. 250   B: Rs. 120   C: Rs. 135   D: Rs. 210

20. If we multiply 90,009 by 909 then digit at the unit place of the product will be …..

21. Hikers at Deer Creek Park

Distance in Miles	Number of Hikers
0–3	50
4–6	35
7–9	25
10–12	10
13–15	20

What length hike did most hikers take? How many people hiked 10–12 miles?

22. What digit will be there at unit's place if we multiply 9, 109, 2009 and 3109?

23. A wall mount clock strikes 4 bells in 4 seconds. It will strike 10 bells in … seconds.

24. What least number should be subtracted from a four digit greatest number to obtain a number divisible by 2 and 4 leaving remainder 1 in each case?

4. Assignments

Exercise 1

1: Following data sheet records number of items sold in an Electronic shop.

Week	Number	Week	Number	Week	Number
1	38	6	28	11	17
2	36	7	25	12	15
3	29	8	19	13	18
4	30	9	23	14	21
5	31	10	20	15	23

In what fraction of the weeks did the number of items sold range from 30 to 40?

Write your answer in simplest form of decimal.

2. How many three digit numbers are there in all?

3. What fraction of all numbers from 1 to 100 are mulltiples of 5?

4. Following data sheet records temperature of certain place (in ^{0}F).

Day	Temperature	Day	Temperature
1	90	6	79
2	86	7	82
3	91	8	76
4	94	9	83
5	88	10	90

In what fraction of the days did the temperature range from 79 °F to 89 °F ?

5. Ritika recrded letters received in her office.

	Sunday	Monday	Tuesday	Wednesday	Thursday	Friday	Saturday
Letters	17	23	12	15	25	7	13

What is the average letters received by herduring the week?

6. Number of messages received by Smita is recorded as follows.

	Sun.	Mon.	Tues.	Wed.	Thur.	Fri.	Sat.
No.of Messages	47	54	26	35	17	85	88

Write the numbers of messages in order from least to greatest.

7. $P = 518.49 \times 7$; $Q = 518.056 + 7$ $\qquad R = 518.749 \div 7$; $S = 518.154 - 7$;

Arrange values of P, Q , R and S in ascending order.

8. What fraction of all the numbers from 1 to 30 are rime numbers?

9. Loxy and Foxy are domesticated cats. Jointly they weigh 16 lb. Loxy weighs half lb more than Foxy, and each cat weighs more than 7 pounds. How much could each cat weigh?

10. Quarter of A, $5/9^{th}$ of B, $6/11^{th}$ of C, $11/13^{th}$ of D are equal to each other. Find out simplest value of the following:

$$\left[\frac{(A + B)(B + C)(C + D)(D + A)}{64\,ABCD} \right] \times \left(\frac{1}{A} + \frac{1}{B} + \frac{1}{C} + \frac{1}{D} \right)$$

11. $1/13^{th}$ of a number exceeds smallest number of five digits by 1001. Find out the number. Also find out seventh multiple of that number.

Exercise 2

1: Following tablr shows record of favorit colours of students of a class.

R G Y Y B P B R G Y Y B P B P B P G Y R G R G Y Y B P B
P R R R Y G B P B P G Y R G R G Y Y B P B R G Y Y B P B
P B P G Y R G R G Y Y B P B R G Y Y B P B R G Y Y B P B

R = red;   P = pink;   B = blue;   Y = yellow;   G = green

What fraction of students chose red or blue as their favorite color?

2. Rijuana came home from market at 5:45 P.M. She sent 2 and half hour in market, quarter of one hour in park and three fourth of one hour with friends. By what time did she leave home for market?

3. What fraction of all the natural numbers from 1 to 500 are common multiples of 5 and 25?

4. Which smallest number of six digits is divisible exactly by 3 and 9 leaving remainder 2 in each case. Calculate simplest value of $3/4^{th}$ of that number.

5. Instead of subtracting 123.125 from a number Snehal added 125.123 to it. Find out total difference of her result and the actual result.

6. $\left[\left(1 + \frac{1}{2}\right)\left(1 + \frac{1}{3}\right) \ldots\ldots \left(1 + \frac{1}{10,000}\right) \times \left(5 - \frac{5}{10001}\right)\right] \times 25 \times 8 \ = \ldots$

7. Number of students attended a game session is recorded.

Days	M	T	W	Th	F
No. of Students	52	75	98	80	100

Number of students recorded in the roll is 200. Write attendance of students of each days in fractions and decimals.

Exercise 3

1: What fraction of all the natural numbers from 1 to 600 are common multiples of 15 and 30?

2. $\left(\dfrac{1}{2} X \dfrac{2}{3} X \dfrac{3}{4} X \dots \dfrac{9,999}{10,000}\right) X \dfrac{1}{10,000} X 10^p = 1$; here p = ...

3. Fractions having numerator 1 are called ………. fractions.

4. Three fourth of four eleventh of a number is equal to 30,30,303. Find out the natural number.

5. Represent all of the following by using suitable number sentences.

a. 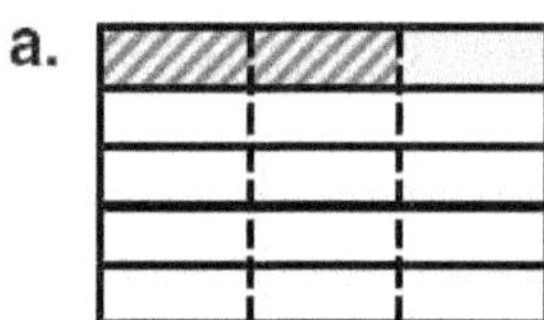
b. 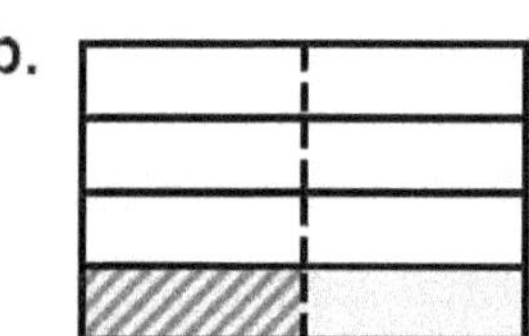
c. 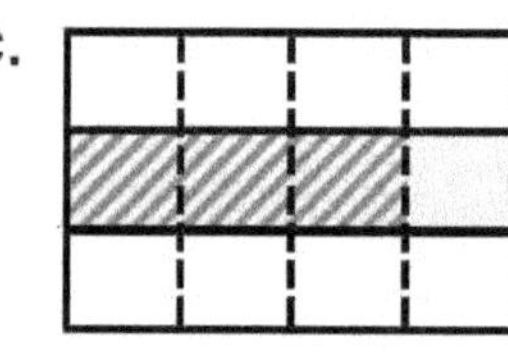
d. 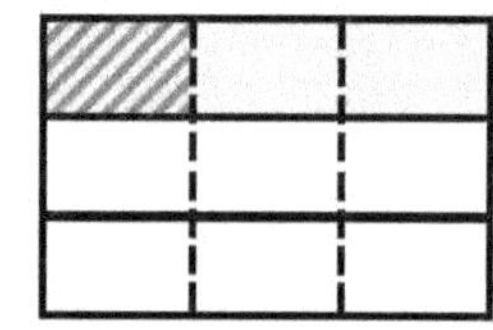

6. Namrata observed that cistern A, B and C are taking 20 minutes, 40 minutes and one hour respectively to refill $3/4^{th}$ of a water tank. If all the three cisterns kept open then time taken by these cisterns to fill up the water tank completely will be ……………

7. Anamika can finish half of a project activity in 6 days, three fourth of that work will be completed by Snehal in 8 days. If they work jointly to finish the project work then the work will be complete by them in ……. days.

8. $(1 + 2 + \dots\dots 50,000) X 25,000 X (49,999 + 2)^{-1} = 5^p \, 10^q$; here p/q = …

9. How many five digit numbers are there in all? What fraction of all such numbers are divisible by 25?

10. Three angles of a triangle are in the ratio of $\dfrac{1}{2} : \dfrac{1}{3} : \dfrac{1}{4}$. Find out magnitude of all the three interior angles of that triangle.

11. If $11/19^{th}$ of a natural number is equal to 38,57,076. Find out the number.

Exercise 4

1: one third of angle A, one fourth of B and $1/5^{th}$ of C are equal to each other. Find out all the interior angles.

2. $7/11^{th}$ of a number is equal to $9/13^{th}$ of another number. Find out ratio of both the numbers.

3. Half of A, quarter of B, $4/5^{th}$ of C and $5/7^{th}$ of D are equal to each other. Find out ratio of A, B, C and D.

4. Calculate portion of grid which is not shaded.

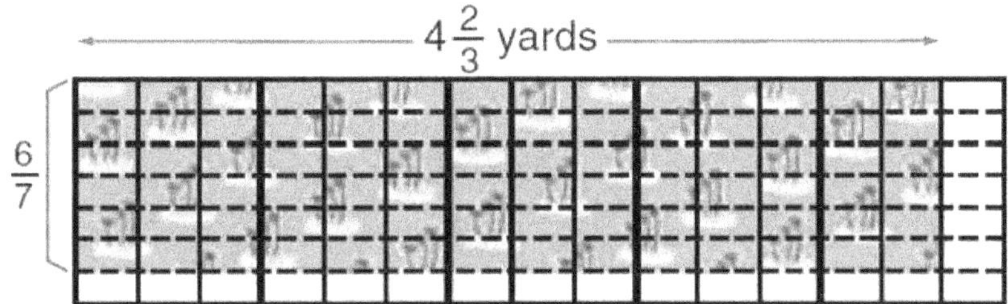

5. $\frac{1}{2}\ of\ \frac{2}{3}of\ \frac{3}{11}\ of\ p = 10,20,300.$ Find out simplest value of p.

6. Represent shaded portions in the following grid by using fraction.

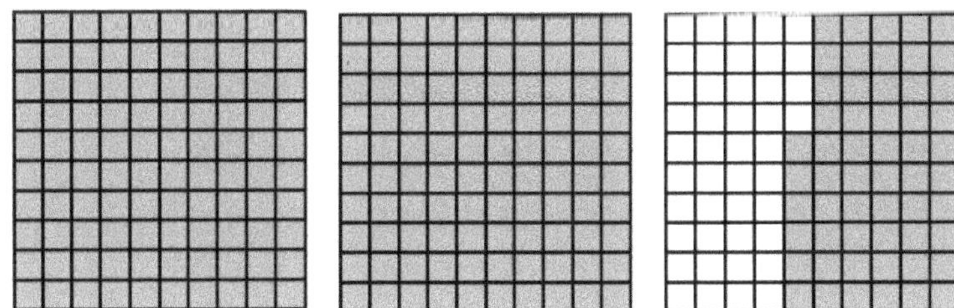

7. Use the place value chart to represent 2041.935

1,000	100	10	1	0.1	0.01	0.001
Thousands	Hundreds	Tens	Ones	Tenths	Hundredths	Thousandths

Exercise 5

Compare the following:

1. 3,505 = _______________

3,055 = _______________

3,505 ◯ 3,055

2. 7.15 = _______________

17.5 = _______________

7.15 ◯ 147.5

3. 42.8 = _______________

42.80 = _______________

42.8 ◯ 42.80

4. 0.025 = _______________

0.250 = _______________

0.025 ◯ 0.250

5. 8,296 = _______________

596 = _______________

8,296 ◯ 596

6. 4,000,976 = _______________

4,009,076 = _______________

4,000,976 ◯ 4,009,076

7: Three box pack and another three fourth of cakes are to be distributed equally amongst 15 friends. Calculate part of cakes which will be shared by each of the friends.

8. Somnath prepares a project activity in 15 days while working 4 hours a day. He preferred working 2 and half hours a day. Calculate total number of days to be taken by him to finish the project works.

9. $(1 + 2 + \ldots. 20{,}000) \times 10{,}000 \times (9{,}999 + 2)^{-1} = 2^p \, 5^q$; here p/q = …

10. One third of the class is divided into 9 equal groups. What part of the class is each group?

11. Three fourths of a squad is divided into 12 teams. What part of the squad is each team?

Exercise 6

1: What least number should be added to $5/9^{th}$ of product of greatest and smallest number of five digits to make the number divisible exactly by 9?

2. $(1 + 2 + 3 + \dots 60{,}000) \times 30{,}000 \times (59{,}999 + 2)^{-1} = 9 \times 10^{p}$; $p = \dots..$

3. What least number should be added to sum of three digit and four digit greatest numbers to obtain a common multiple of 3 and 9?

4. Camilo has 3.5 hour to solve 70 math problems. If he spends the same amount of time on each problem, what part of an hour does he spend on each problem? How many problems could be solved by him in half of an hour?

5. $1/9^{th}$ of $3/13^{th}$ of a number exceeds smallest five digit number by 101. Find the number.

6. Tank A is filled u by cistern P completely in 40 minutes, cistern Q can take 20 minutes to fill up one fifth of the tank. Tank B is filled up completely by both the cisterns jointly in 45 minutes. Calculate total time to be taken by both the cisterns to fill up tank A and tank B completely.

7. What least number should be added to smallest odd number of six digits to make the number a common multiple of 3, 6, 99 and 12.

8. What least number should be subtracted from six digit greatest number to obtain a number exactly divisible by 8?

9. How many six digit numbers are there in all?

10. 20% of 70% of a natural number is equal to 14,28,042. Find out the number.

11. What least number should be subtracted from thousands place of 32,98,128 to obtain a common multiple of 3 and 9?

12. Round to the nearest tenth: (a) 67.01   (b) 12.021   (c) 29.891.

13. Out of 25 householders 16 have a dog and 12 have a cat. Five people have both a cat and a dog. How many of the householders have only dogs?

14. $13/29^{th}$ of a number is equal to 26,26,039. Find out the number.

Exercise 7

1: Identify pair of angles in the following on the basis of their properties.

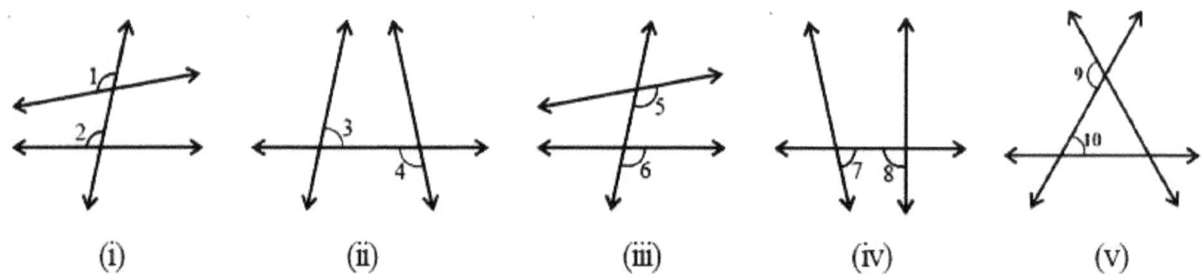

(i)   (ii)   (iii)   (iv)   (v)

2. Complete the following.

3. Sum of complementary and supplementary angles of a given angle is equal to 150^0. Find out the angle.

4. Which smallest number of seven digits is divisible exactly by 9?

5. How many six digit numbers are there in all?

6. A light is placed at the top of table above 40 cm. light reaches at the edge of table by crossing a distance of 50 cm. Find out radius of the circular table.

7. In a given expression $(x^2 - x + 1) = 0$. By using this relationship find out value of x.

8. Sum of a number and three times of its reciprocal is equal to 4. Find out sum of square, cube and third multiple of that number.

9. What least number should be subtracted from fifth multiple of 10,001 to obtain a common multiple of 5 and 25?

10. During the last 4 weekends, Nikita has volunteered for 2.5 hours, 1.7 hours, 3.1 hours, and 1.5 hours respectively. For about how long has she volunteered in the last 4 weekends?

11. Snehal can finish her project works in 6 days while working 5 hours a day. She preferred increasing her daily engagement by one hour. Calcculate number of days she could save in this way.

Exercise 8

1: A spinner has 3 equal sections that are white, yellow, and green. Another spinner has 3 equal sections that are blue, purple, and red. How many different combinations of colors are possible if you spin each spinner once?.

2. Roshni wants to sit by her four sisters at the school assembly. How many different ways can they sit together along one row?

3. Find out sum of all the interior angles of a pentagon.

4. How many diagonals will be there in a pentagon which can be drawn passing through a definite vertex?

5. Is it possible to draw a triangle by using sides 3 cm, 4 cm and 8 cm?

6. Is it possible to have a quadrilateral with two reflex angles? At most how many obtuse angles could be there in a quadrilateral.

7. What least number of three digit should be added to smallest seven digit numbers to obtain a common multiple of 3 and 9?

8. Roshni is making a pizza for dinner. She has mushrooms, onions, potato and pineapple to put on the pizza. How many different pizzas can Selena make with toppings?

9. Stevensons went shopping and spent a total of Rs. 240 on meat for dinners for the week. They purchased chicken for Rs. 30 per pound and some hamburger for Rs 24 per pound. They spent five times as much money on chicken as on hamburger. How many pounds of chicken and how many pounds of hamburger did the family purchase?

10. What fraction of 12321 is equal to 111?

11. What least number should be added to five digit greatest number to make it divisible by 9 leaving a remainder 5?

12. Robert lives $4\frac{3}{10}$ miles from school. Timothi lives $\frac{21}{5}$ miles from school. Who lives farther from school? How much farther?

13. Rina did a survey of how much time students spend on homework each night. Out of 16 people interviewed, ½ spend about 1 hour on homework and ¼ spend about 45 minutes on homework. The rest spend about 30 minutes on homework. How many students spend ½ hour on homework?

Exercise 9

1: Convert the following expression into an equivalent fraction.

  a: 20 tenths + 203 hundredths + 2,005 thousandths + 12 tenths

  b: $15/19^{th}$ of 19,019 + $11/13^{th}$ of 13,013 + $16/33^{rd}$ of 33,033 = ………………

  c: Half of 500 multiplied by 625 and again multiplied by 1,000

2: Sum total of a number and its reciprocal is equal to 8.125. Find the number.

3: Somalia converted six digit greatest multiple of 4 into a common multiple of 5, 10 and 15 by subtracting …………….. from it. (Consider it as a smallest possible number.).

4: Is there any pair of number having LCM 12321 and HCF 1690?

5: What least number can be subtracted from the greatest even number of six digits to obtain a multiple of 6?

6: Sum total of five consecutive numbers is equal to third multiple 150,005. Find sum total of smallest and greatest numbers of this number series.

7: Rohit can finish half of a wall painting in 12 days and Mohan can finish quarter of the same painting in 4 days. They started working jointly to finish 7 such wall paintings. They can finish their works in ……….. days.

8: A train can cross a light post in 1 m 4 seconds while moving with a uniform speed of 72 km/h. Find time to be taken by this train to cross a tunnel of length 5 km 60 m.

9: Sneha reduced her consumption of fuel by 20% to balance price rise of fuel. Calculate the percentage increase of cost of fuel by using the above data.

10: After incorporating Joseph in a team of 11 students of average height 1 m 6 cm the average age is increased by 12 cm. Find height of John.

11: How many vertices, edges and corners are there in a pentagonal prism?

12: If square tables are arranged in a restaurant so that only one person can sit on any side of the table, how many tables will it take to seat 40 people?

Exercise 10

1: What fraction of all the numbers starting from 1 to 1,000 are multiples of 25?

2: Write three fractions which can be placed in between 1/3 and ¼ on a number line.

3. Half of a quarter of a number exceeds eighth multiple of 300,003 by 72. Find the number.

4: Radius of a square sized playground is equal to 21 m. Mohini completes her daily practice of jogging by encircling around it for four times. Find total distance covered by Mohini during her daily jogging.

5: A cistern can fill up a water tank in 45 minutes another cistern takes 1 h 30 m to fill up the same water tank. Both the tanks kept open to fill up the water tank. Time taken by both the cisterns jointly to fill up the water tank will be …………………..

6: [(5.5 + 5.05 + 5.005 + 5.0005 + 5.00005 + 5.000005) – 25] ÷ 5 = ……..

7: Cost of half a dozen banana is equal to Rs 40. Cost of 50 bananas will be Rs.

8: Rijuana travels 20 m in a couple of seconds by using her car. Mohini travels by using her car with an average speed of 76 km/h. They started jointly from the origin and a gap developed in between them after half an hour. Calculate the gap developed in between them as they were travelling in the same direction.

9: Calculate the least possible time interval after which three bells toll together. These bells toll at an interval of 10 seconds, 15 seconds and 20 seconds respectively.

Write each decimal as a fraction in simplest form.

10. 0.9	11. 0.07	12. 0.43	13. 0.77
14. 0.003	15. 0.127	16. 0.45	17. 0.36

18. How many three digit numbers can be made by using digits 2, 5 and 9 only once in each case?

19. $2/9^{th}$ of $9/11^{th}$ of $11/13^{th}$ of a natural number is equal to 20,40,008. Find out the number.

20. Observe the rate with which following pattern of plantation is growing.

```
n = 1           n = 2                n = 3                      n = 4

X X X          X X X X X            X X X X X X X              X X X X X X X X X X
X ● X          X ●    ● X           X ●    ●    ● X           X ●   ●    ●    ● X
X X X          X        X           X            X            X                   X
               X ●    ● X           X ●    ●    ● X           X ●   ●    ●    ● X
               X X X X X            X            X            X                   X
                                    X ●    ●    ● X           X ●   ●    ●    ● X
                                    X X X X X X X             X                   X
                                                             X ●   ●    ●    ● X
      X = conifer tree                                       X                   X
      ● = apple tree                                         X ●   ●    ●    ● X
                                                             X X X X X X X X X X
```

Complete the following table:

n	Number of apple trees	Number of conifer trees
1	1	8
2	4	……
3	……	24
4	16	32
5	……	……

As the farmer makes the orchard bigger, which will increase more quickly: the number of apple trees or the number of conifer trees?

21. What digit will be there at ones place if we multiply 8008 by 10,008?

22. A natural number exceeds fifth multiple of five digit smallest number by 5,005. Find out the number.

5. Question Bank

Set 1

1: What fraction of all the natural numbers starting from 1 to 400 are multiples of 20?

2. $\left(\frac{1}{2} \ X \ \frac{2}{3} \ X \ \frac{3}{4} \ ....\ ... \ \frac{9999}{10000} \right) \ X \ 27 = \ \sqrt[4]{p} \ X \ 10^q$; here p = …. and q = …

3. one tenth X 6 hundredth X 10,000 + 1.0324 = …………

4. One fifth of one sixth of 60,30,090 = ……………..

5. 3/49 of a natural number is equal to 30,30,300. Find the number.

6. Four fifth of A is equal to five sixth of B. Find simple ratio of A and B. Also represent such ratio in three equivalent fractions.

7. Five sixths of the books on the shelf are nonfiction. $1/18^{th}$ of the books are mathematics. Three fourths of rest of the books are science books. What part of the books on the shelf are science books?

8. Who is moving with greater speed?

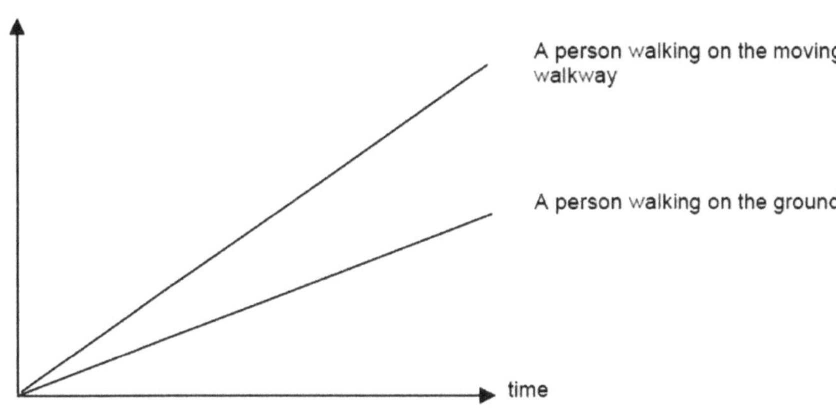

Set 2

1: Using each of the digits 2, 3, 5, and 7 only once, find two fractions that will have a product n such that:

A: It is a product close to 1.

B: It is a maximum possible product of both the fractions.

C: It is a minimum possible product of both the fractions.

2. One third of the 24 students in class read books on sports. How many students in the class do not read books on sports?

3. What fraction of all the numbers starting from 1 to 500 are multiples of 25?

4. Seven eleventh of a natural number is equal to 70,70,707. Find out the natural number.

5. How many three digit numbers can be obtained if we use digits 2, 3 and 0 only once? What will be the product of greatest and smallest such number?

6. A passenger train takes 54 seconds to cross a light post while moving by maintaining an average speed of 18 km/h. What is the length of that train?

7. Two trains cross each other completely while moving through up and down track in 2 minutes 32 seconds. Average speed of both the trains are 18 km/h and 36 km/h respectively. Find out total length of both the trains. If ratio of both the length is 3:2 and train having greater seed is longer, then calculate length both the trains.

8. A wall mount clock spends 3 seconds for striking three bells at 3 a.m. calculate total time to be taken by this clock to strike 9 bells at 9 a. m. and 11 bells at 11 a. m.

9. What percentage of all the natural numbers from 1 to 625 are multiples of 25?

10. What smallest number should be subtracted from smallest eight digit numbers to obtain one third of greatest seven digit number?

11. $3/7^{th}$ of $7/19^{th}$ of a natural number exceeds third multiple of 10,001. Find out the number.

Set 3

1: What least number should be multiplied to 121,000 to make the product divisible by 1,331?

2. There are 40 members in a basketball team which is finalised for the forthcoming season. Three fifths are fifth-grade students. One tenth are class six students. Rest of the others are seniors. How many members of the basketball team are senior students?

3. A cistern can fill up half of a water tank in 15 minutes, it can fill up another water tank in 45 minutes. Calculate total time to be taken by this cistern to fill up both the tanks completely.

4. Rikin formed greatest and smallest four digit numbers without repeating any of the digits. Find out sum of both the numbers.

5. What fraction of all the numbers starting from 1 to 600 are multiples of 30?

6. Half of one seventh of a natural number exceeds seven digit smallest number by 1,001. Find out the number.

7. 1,2091 X 125 X 25 X 40 X 8 = ………………….

8. 144 students were standing in the assembly in such a way that number of rows and number of students in each row is equal. How many students are there in each row?

9. 293 marbles are there. Six friends wanted to share these marbles equally. How many marbles each of them will get? How many marbles remain undivided?

[share of each friend = 48; marbles left = 5]

10. In certain office one third all workers are women. 16/17th of all the working women are married. If number of unmarried women in the office is 10 then find the total number of men working in that office.

11. Mr Somalwar got an assignment of solving 12 sums in 10 minutes and 16 other sums in 12 minutes. If a set of questions containing 4 sums of first type and 8 sums of second type then he can finish that paper in ______ minutes.

Set 4

1: How many seven digit numbers are there in all?

2. $(1099 \times 209 \times 3099 \times 4009 \times 30909) = p$; if we write numerical value of p in standard form then digit at the unit place will be ....

3. Which seven digit smallest number is a common multiples of 3 and 9?

4. Celia had 4 and half yards of ribbon in her scrap box. She used half of it for her project. Half of the remaining is given to her friend. Find out length of the ribbon which were not used.

5. Half of a number A, quarter of B and one sixth of C are equal to each other. Find out simplest ratio of A, B and C. Also find out the simplest value of $\left(\dfrac{A^3 + B^3 + C^3}{3ABC}\right)$.

6. What least number should be subtracted from the product of four digit greatest number and four digit smallest number to obtain a common multiple of 3 and 9?

7. Complete the following number series.

$(1 + 3 + 5 + 7)$	=	4×4	=	16;
$(1 + 3 + 5 + \ldots + 11)$	=	... X	=	36;
(Sum of 20 consecutive odds)	=	... X	=	.....;
(Sum of 100 consecutive odds)	=	... X	=	.....;

8. What lest number should be subtracted from greatest five digit numbers to obtain a common multiple of 3, 6 and 9?

9. What digit will be there at unit place of the product of 9, 209, 3099 and 8089?

10. A daily wager takes half an hour in between two engagements of a couple of hours each. Find out the maximum possible engagements in his nine hour long engagement at the job site.

11. Find a smallest possible number of five digits divisible by 4, 6, 8 and 12 leaving remainder 3 in each case.

Set 5

1: Divide greatest six digit number by greatest two digit number. Add 11 to the result and again multiply 125 and 8 to it. What are the digits at ones and tens place of your result?

2. $(1 + 2 + ... + 1000) \times 500 \times 125 \times 8 \times 40 = 1001 \times 10^p$. Here $p = ...$

3. What fraction of all the natural numbers starting from 1 to 1000 are multiples of 125?

4. A cistern takes 15 minutes to fill up quarter of tank A, One fifth of tank B and one seventh of tank C. Calculate total time to be taken by the cistern to fill up all the tanks completely.

5. $1/11^{th}$ of $1/9^{th}$ of a number is equal to 10,10,100. Find out the number.

6. A shopkeeper gains an amount equal to SP of 1 apple by selling 11 apples. Find out total gain percentage made by the shopkeeper.

7. 20% of 30% of a number is equal to tenth multiple of 1,001. Find it.

8. Observe the following numbers represented in expanded form.

    30,550   = 50 + _____a_____ + 500

    809,100   = 800,000 + 100 + _____b__

    725,608   = 20,000 + 700,000 + 8 + _c__ + 5,000

Statements ---

I: Numbers are represented in the International System. II: All a, b and c are in thousands.

III: Sum total of a, b and c exceeds 60,000.   IV: In ascending order c > b > a.

Which of the statements are true?

A: I, II and IV   B: Only IV   C: None

9. $21/29^{th}$ of a given number is equal to 21,21,063. Find ut the number.

Set 6

1: A table lam is installed at the top of a study table in such a way that the light falling on the circular table covers up the table up to the edge. Edge of the table is at a distance of 6 ft from the light and is at a distance of 3 ft from the center of the table. Find out the vertical height of the light in relation to the table.

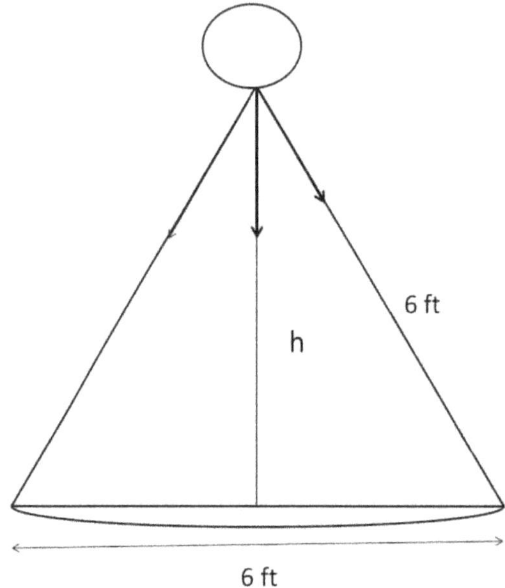

2. Digit at unit place of the product of 199, 989, 10899 , 989 and 129 is ………...

3. Product of 125, 8, 625 and 129 is represented in standard form. Digit at tens place in that presentation will be ……...

4. Light from a celestial body reaches the earth in eight minutes 16 seconds. Light travels six lakh km in a couple of second. Represent the distance of that celestial body from the earth by using a scientific notation.

5. Two cisterns fill up a water tank separately in 40 minutes and 1 hour respectively. Calculate total time taken by both the cisterns to fill up three such water tanks jointly.

6. $P = 11.01 + 11.001 + 101.101 + 102.003 - 225$;

$Q = 24.01 + 24.001 + 204.101 + 204.003 - 456$;

Calculate : $\left(\dfrac{1}{P} - \dfrac{1}{Q}\right)(P + Q + 121\,P + 213\,Q)(P^2 - Q^2)$

7. Calculate area of the following.

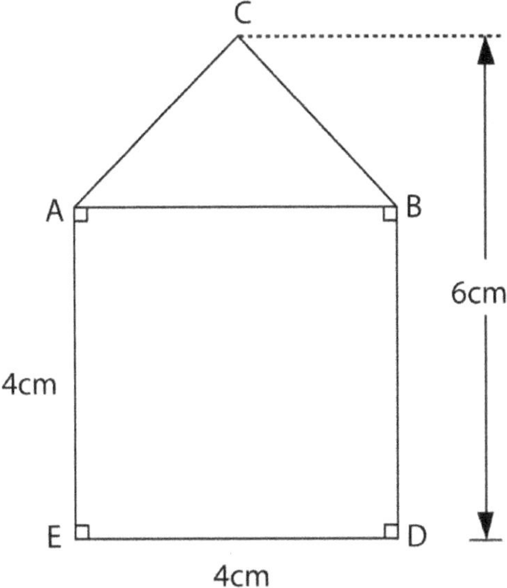

8. Compare area of shaded portions.

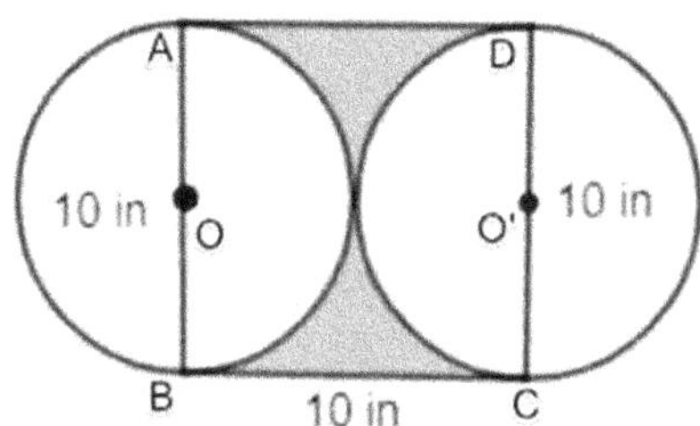

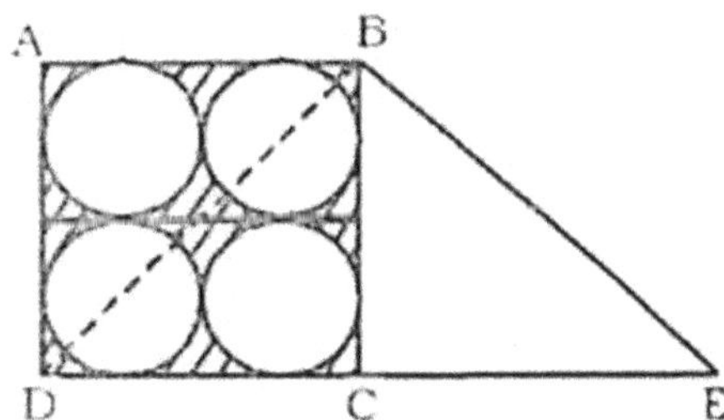

Diagram P   Diagram Q

Set 7

1: Calculate and compare parts of grid which are shaded.

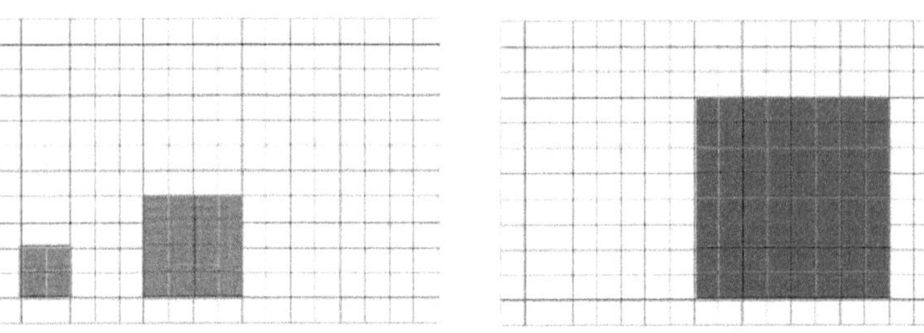

Grid A   Grid B

2. How many six digit numbers are there in all?

3. P = 30% of 300,300; Q = 40% of 400,400 And R = 50% of 500,500.

$$(P + Q + R) \div \left(1 + \frac{1}{1000}\right) = \dots\dots\dots$$

4. If the given pattern continues then un-shaded beads at 17th level will be equal to

....

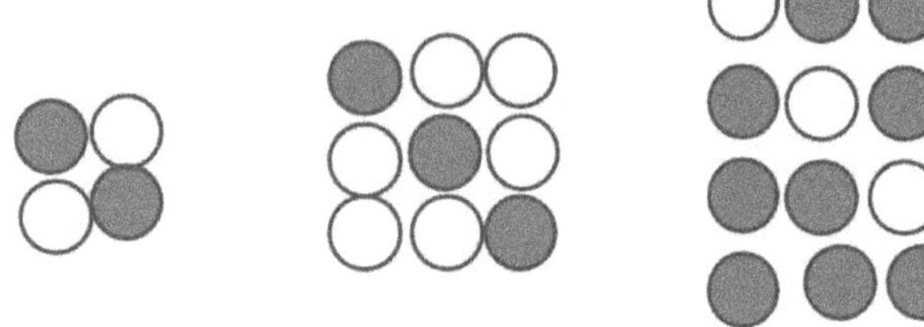

1st Pattern   2nd Pattern   3rd Pattern

5. How many more six digit numbers are there than five digit numbers?

6. If we multiply 9.009, 1.001, 2.002, 125, 40, 8 and 40 then number of decimal places in the product will be …………

7. 20% of 50% of 200,300,400 = …………..

8. How many times des 7 occur if we write all the numbers starting from 1 to 100?

9. Represent the following by using fractions.

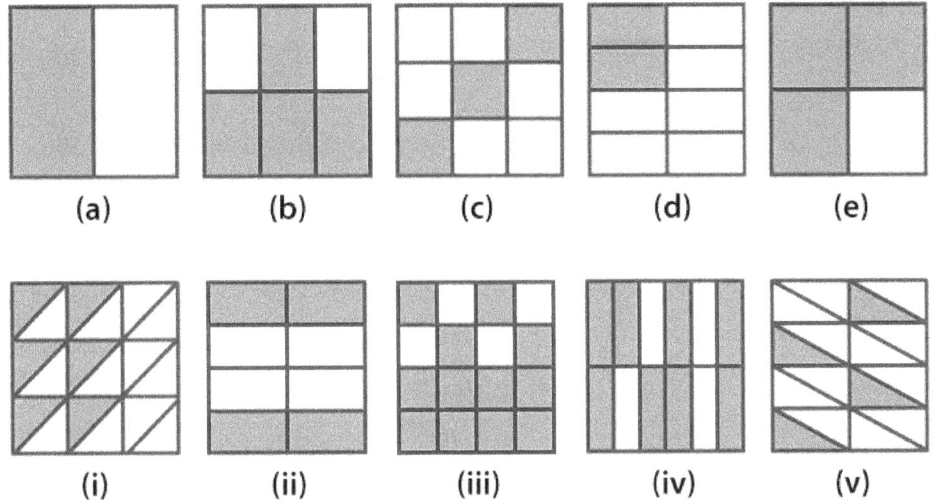

10. What least number should be subtracted from 329,089,743 to make it divisible by 4?

11. Calculate area of shaded portion.

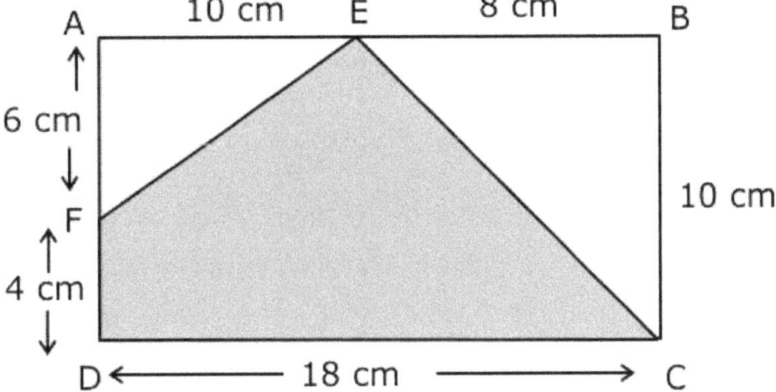

12. What least number should be added to tens place of 32,421 to make the number divisible by 3 and 9?

13. 20% of a number exceeds fifth myltiple of five digit smallest number by 5005. Find out the number.

14: A scanner (along with scanning operator) requires six mnths to scan 198,198 books completely. Equal books are scanned Everyday by the scanner. What number of books is scanned in a month?

15. While dividing a number by 121 a student obtained 100,100,100. There was no remainder. What was the number?

16. There were 20,172 tickets sold for a 3-game tournament series. If the same number of tickets was sold for each game, then find out how many tickets were sold for each of the games?

17. Mohini collected Rs 625 from her class to promote a charity show. Each of the students contributed amount equal to the student strength of that class. How many students are there in the class?

18. There are 378 people going on a field trip. Nine buses are hired for the trip. There will be two passengers extra in sixth bus and a couple of passengers less in fifth bus. If the same number of people rides in rest of the other buses, then find out total people ride in each bus?

19. $(A + B) = 2002$; $(B + C) = 2003$; $(C + A) = 3009$;

   Find out simplest value of $(A + B + C)$.

20. Somalika can finish her assignments in 16 days while working three hours a day. She can finish all her assignments in ….. days while working 4 hours a day.

21. Three bells toll at an interval of 3 seconds, four seconds and six seconds respectively. How many times do all the three bells toll together in 2 h 24 minutes?

22. Speed of car A is 18 km/h and speed of car B is 10 m/s. car B was 2 km away from car A. Smita started her stop watch to record total time taken by car A to overtake car B while moving through the same road. Find out reading of the stop watch.

23. 30% of 50% of 10,20,300 = ………………………

Set 8

1: Average weight of 10 apples estimated as 69 g. Later on it is observed that Weight of each apple is 1.09 g less that the estimated weight. What was the original average weight of apples?

2. P = (1.009 - 1.009 + 1.009 − 1.009 ….. six hundred times);

Q = (4.991 − 4.991 + 4.991 − 4.991 … seven hundred seven times);

$$P + Q = \ldots\ldots\ldots\ldots$$

3. Represent in decimal form:

$$1009 + \frac{109}{125} + \frac{29}{40} + \frac{193}{250} + \frac{19}{25} + 1.009 + 3.991 + 4.891 + 0.109$$

4. Rajani has a box with 6 marbles numbered from 1 to 6 on each of them. She picks a marble from it without seeing. What is the probability that the marble picked has the number 3 on it?

5. One fifth of a number is equal to 2002 mre than second multiple of 10,001. Find out the given number..

6. 20% of 40% of 50% of 100,300 = …………………

7. Find out values of interior angles in the following.

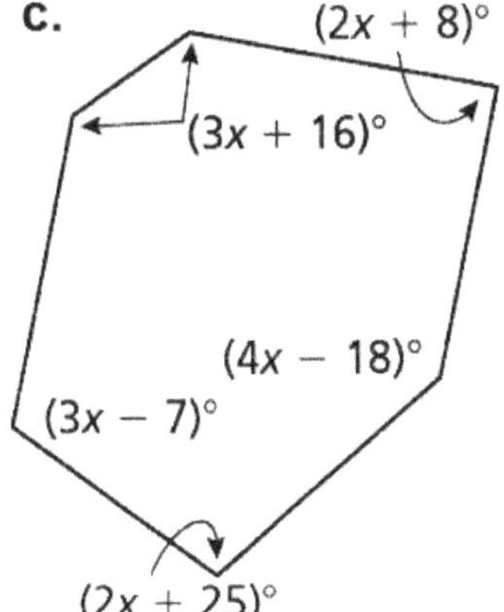

8. What fraction of each of the following grids are shaded?

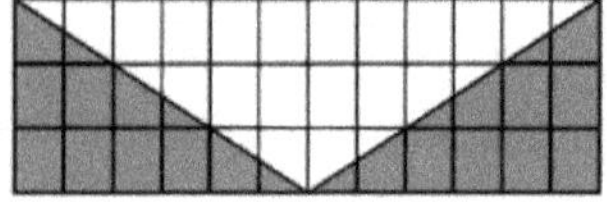

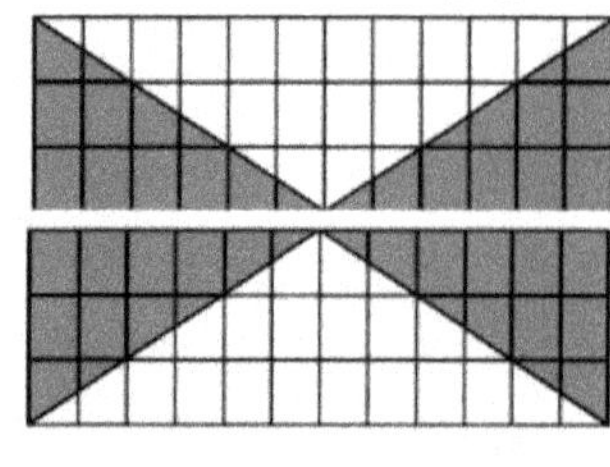

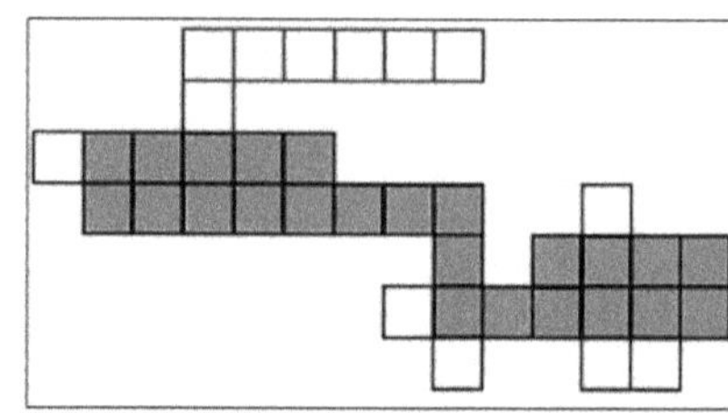

P   Q   R

9. How many additional cells in the following should be shaded to make the figure bilaterally symmetrical?

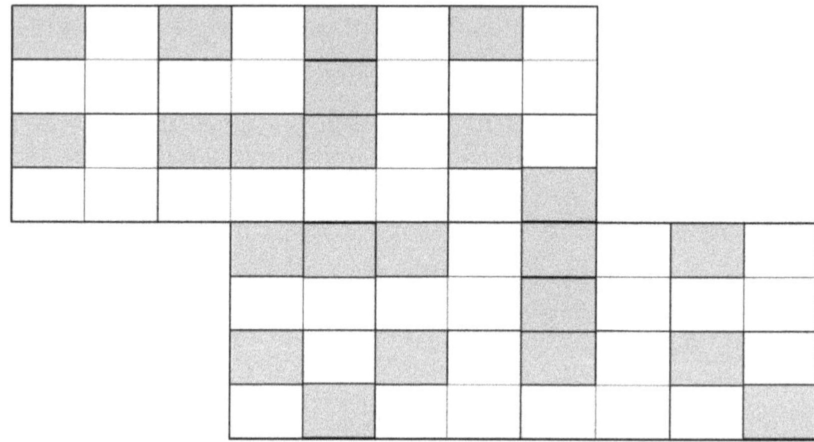

10. P = 1009 X 1125 X 8 X 40 X 25 X 20009 X $\left(1 + \dfrac{1}{1000}\right)$ X $\dfrac{1}{1000}$;

Digit at ones place of P will be ....

11. $(1 + x)(1 + x^2)(1 + x^3) \ldots\ldots (1 + x^{1000}) = 0$; find $(x^{1021} - x^{-921} = \ldots..$

12. Which of the following will form linear pair?

13. What least number should be added to product of greatest three digit number and smallest four digit number to obtain a common multiple of 3 and 9?

14. After selling 22 apples a shopkeeper gained an amount equal to selling price of two apples. Find out his gain percentage.

15. Find angles in the following.

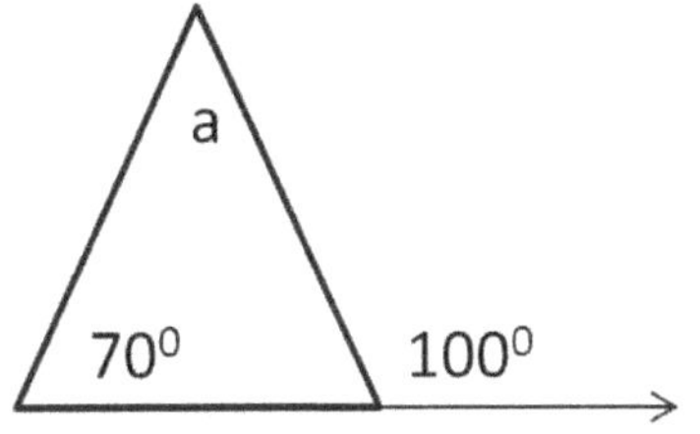

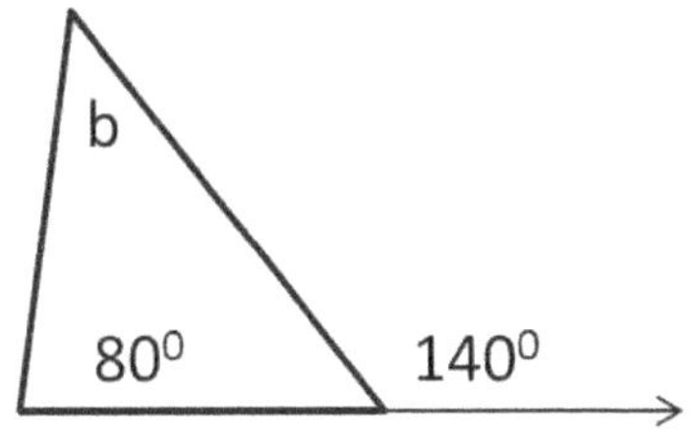

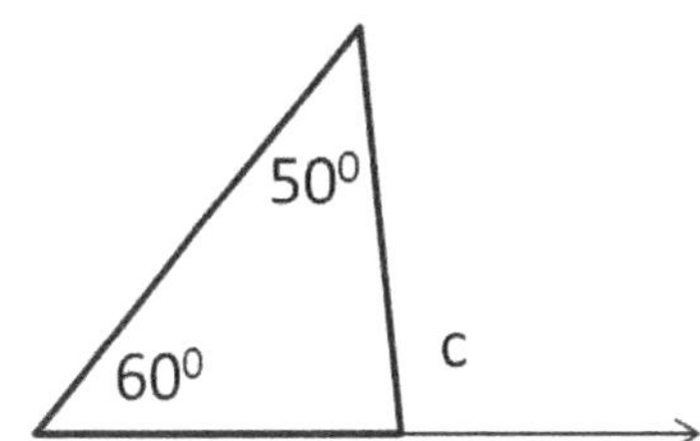

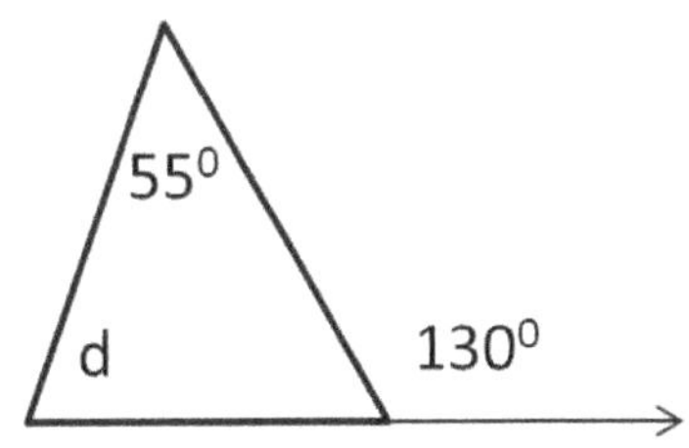

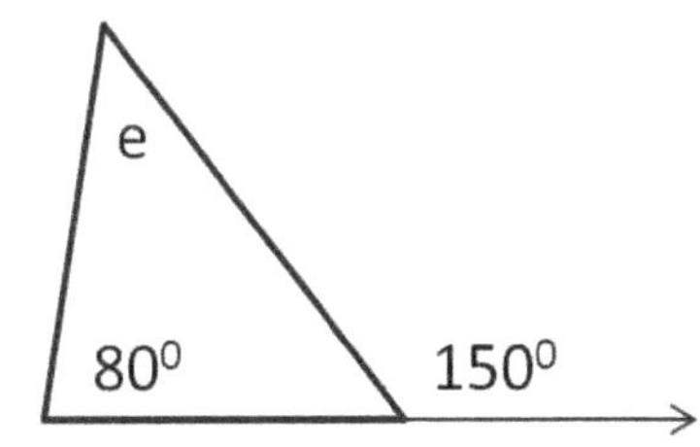

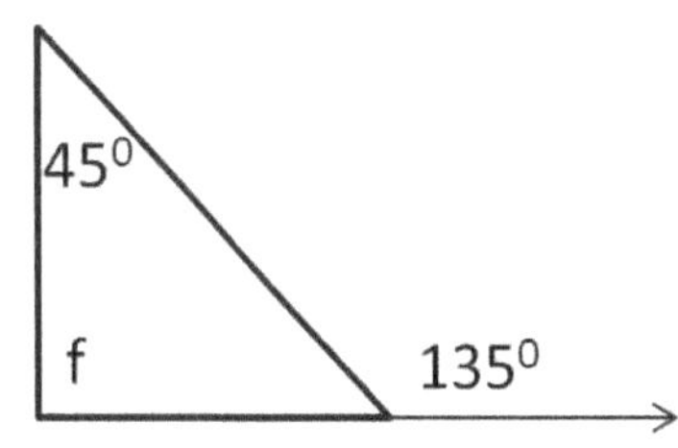

16. After increasing value of a product by 15% a shopkeeper issued 10% discount to all the customers. Calculate the gain percentage.

17. Represent shaded parts by using simple fractions.

18. Observe the given fractions.

a. 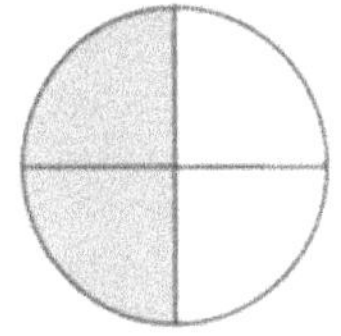
b. 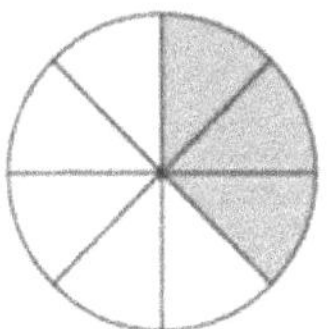
c. 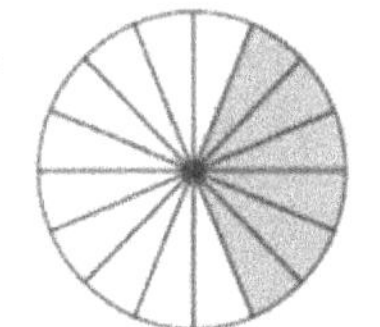
d. 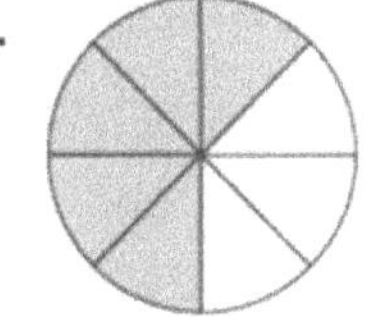

Calculate: (21 a + 12 b + 8 c – 0.02d + 12.009) = ……………

19. Which of the following statements is true?

(A) The mean height of the mountains is greater than their median height.

(B) The mean height of the mountains is less than their mode.

(C) The median height of the mountains is less than their mode.

(D) The median height of the mountains is greater than their mean height.

20. Write in standard form:

$\{(125 \times 40 \times 8 \times 25 + 10^4) \div 10^8\} - 121.0121 = \ldots\ldots\ldots\ldots\ldots$

21: Find out angles.

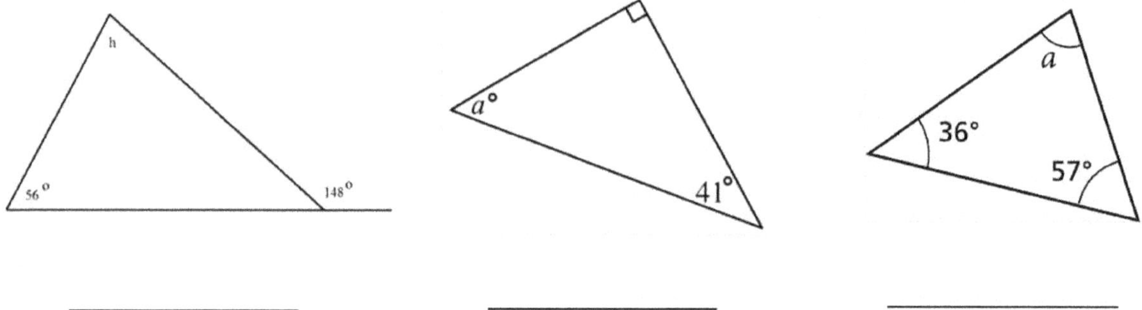

—————   —————   —————

22. Sonalika prepared three counters which produce beats at uniform intervals of 5 seconds, 10 seconds and 15 seconds. After what time intervals do they produce beats together? How many times joint beats will be generated by them in time interval of a couple of hours?

23. 30 men works together to finish a work in 380 days. 27 additional men joined the team to finish the work as early as possible. Calculate total number of days saved by them in this way.

24. A boat moves down the stream in 39 minutes and returns back while moving up-stream in 1 h 21 minutes. Calculate ratio of the speed of the boat and speed of the stream.

25. Equal numbers of square sized tiles are used for the floor of 1331 sq cm. find out maximum possible size of all such square sized tiles.

Set 9

1: What least number should be added to the product of four digit greatest number and four digit smallest number to obtain a common multiple of 3 and 9?

2. 12,43,405 X 125 X 25 X 8 X 40 ÷ 10,000 = ……………..

3. Fifth multiple of 5,005 + 6th multiple of 6,006 = ………………

4. Half of 2,002 + quarter of 4,004 + $1/6^{th}$ of 6,006 = ……. X (999 + 2)

Check divisibility of the following by 11.

5. 133,100`   6. 121,121,121   7. 134,431,000

Check divisibility of the following by 9. Also work out least number to be added to the numbers to make them divisible by 9.

8. 324,543,654   9. 430,435,003   10. 999 X 1001

11. 2 more than the product of greatest and smallest 5 digit numbers.

32. What least number should be subtracted from six digit greatest number to obtain a common multiple of 2, 3, 6 and 9?

33. Half of water tank A, Quarter of B, $1/5^{th}$ of C and $1/6^{th}$ of D are filled up individually by a cistern in 20 minutes. Calculate total time to be taken by that cistern to fill up all the water tanks completely.

34. Three interior angles of a triangle are in the ratio of 2: 3: 6. Find out magnitude of the greatest angle.

35. (1 + 2 + …40,000) X 20,000 X 250 = (39,999 + 2)) X 10^{p} ; p = …..

16. $11/17^{th}$ of 17,34,085 + $5/9^{th}$ of 9,18,045 = ………………….

17. Two bells toll at intervals of 4 seconds and 6 seconds respectively. After what time interal do these bells toll together? How many times these bells toll in an interval of half of an hour?

18. Namrata can finish painting a poster in 8 days while working 5 hours a day. Shen can finish painting the same poster in …. days while working 4 hours a day.

Set 10

1: Half of p, quarter of q and $1/7^{th}$ of r are equal to each other. Find out simplest possible ratio of $(p^3 + q^3 + r^3)$ and 3pqr.

2. Sohanlal prepared a project activity in 6 gays while working 5 hours a day. He preferred working 4 hours a day to complete a couple of such project. Find the number of days needed to finish that project.

3. There are 720 students enrolled in VKV Valley School. If there are 18 classrooms in the school, what is the average number of students in each classroom?

4. Rikin divided 133,112,100 by 11. Find out the quotient.

5. Smita divided 3 and half cakes amongst her 14 friends. Find out fraction of the slice obtained by each of her friend.

6. Pallavi, Snehal, Kamalika and Niharika joined a project activity to complete the same in three days. If they prefer working individually then calculate number of days required to finish their individual projects.

7. By selling 22 apples a shopkeeper gained an amount equal to SP of 2 apples. Calculate percentage of profit gained by the shopkeeper.

8. Roy feeds the birds in the zoo 10,400 ounces of birdseed in one year. How many ounces of birdseed does he feed the birds each week?

9. $(1 + 2 + \ldots\ldots 60{,}000) \times 30{,}000 = 540{,}009 \times 10^{p}$; here p = ……..

30: What least number should be added to a six digit smallest multiple of 3 to obtain a common multiple of 4, 6, 8 and 12?

11: Simplify: $(1.111\ldots + 2.222\ldots + 3.33\ldots.. + 4.444\ldots)$ 10 = ………..

12: Anthony emptied his coin bank and made a bar graph of the numbers of each type of coin. The interval he chose was 5 coins. If the graph showed 5 intervals of quarters, 2 intervals of dimes, 3 intervals of nickels, and 10 intervals of pennies, what was the total amount of money in his bank?

Set 11

1: Calculate outer boundary of the following:

2. We calculate total surface area of a cylinder by using a definite formula.

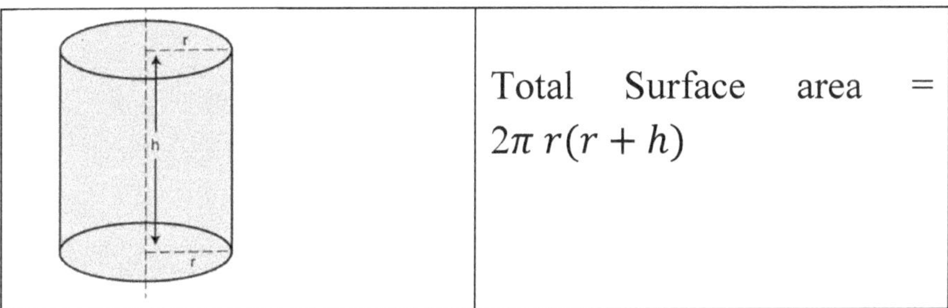

Total Surface area = $2\pi\, r(r + h)$

By using this formula calculate Total Surface Area of the shapes having following specifications.

Sl	Redius of flat face (r)	Height (h)	Total Surface Area (TSA)
1	21	30	
2	35	49	
3	49	58	
4	56	101	

3. The base of a square pyramid has a side length of 27.91 centimeters. The slant height is 25.04 centimeters. Find the surface area.

4. Represent the following in decimal form:

$$154 + \frac{121}{125} + \frac{7}{8} + \frac{39}{40} + \frac{101}{120} + \frac{209}{25}$$

5. How many five digit numbers are there in all ?

6. A passenger train spends 1 m 9 second in crossing a person standing on 2 km 29 m long platform while moving at an average speed of 18 km/h. Calculate total length of the train. Calculate time taken by that train to cross the platform.

7. Compare area of two given triangles in unit square.

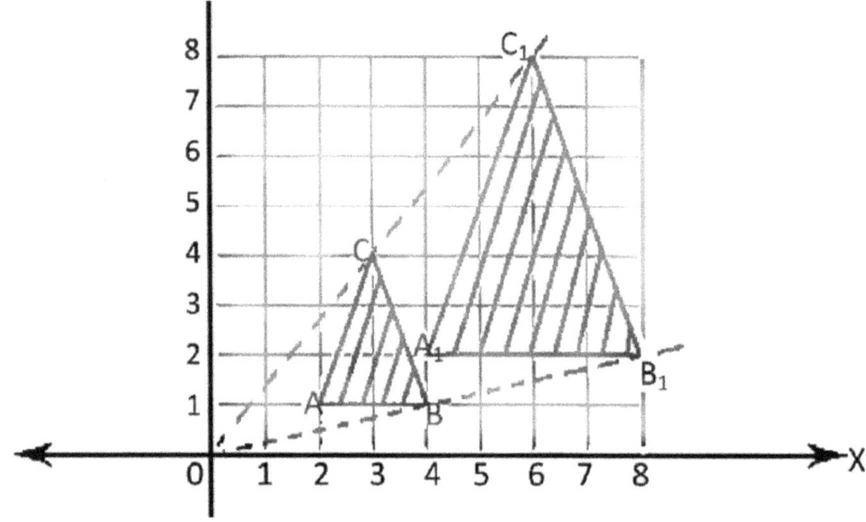

8. Find out unknown angles

Second angle of a right triangle is half of the first angle.

9. Two poles cast shadow on ground up to a definite point. Part of both the shadows superimposed upon each other by part. All lengths displayed in the given figure are on foot. Calculate length of the longer shadow.

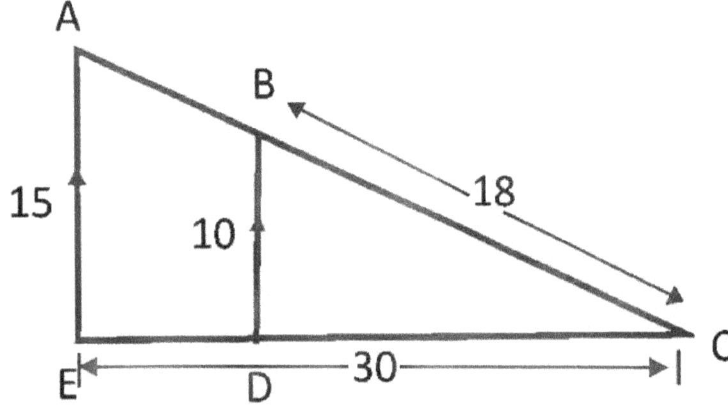

10. Establish relationship in between RW and VB on the basis of the diagram as given.

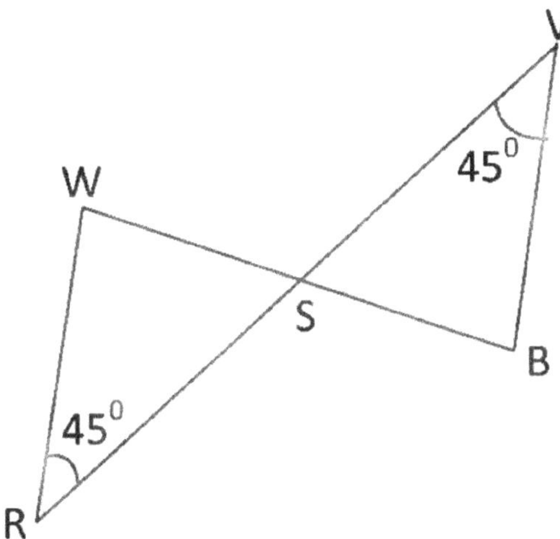

11. Two angles given to construct a triangle are $45^0 45$' and $39^0 39$' . Find out the measure of third angle of that triangle.

12. AC ∥ ED and sides are maintaining a definite ratio. Line segment AE and CD intersects each other at point B. On the basis of given diagram calculate length of DE.

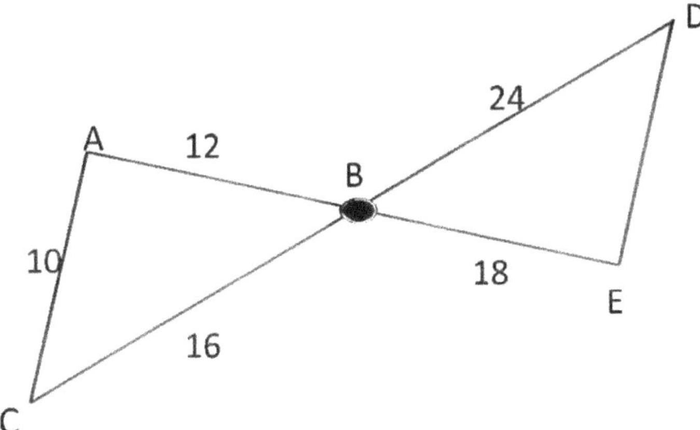

13. Calculate BC: EF = …………

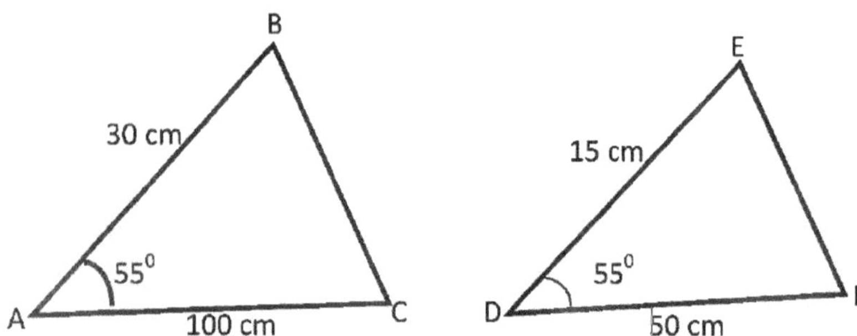

14. After increasing cost of a product by 20% a shopkeeper offered 20% discount on the same product to customers. Find out his total gain or loss percentage.

15. A three digit number prepared in such a way that sum of digits at ones place and hundreds place is equal to digit at tens place. After increasing digit at ones place by 3 it becomes equal to the digit present at hundreds place. Find out the number.

16. The sides of a polygon have lengths 5, 7, 8, 11 and 19 cm. The perimeter of a similar polygon is 150 cm. Find the lengths of the sides of larger polygon.

17. A side of a regular six - sided polygon is 12 cm long. The perimeter of a similar polygon is 90 cm. What is the length of a side of the larger polygon?

18. The ratio of the sides of two similar polygon is 3:2. The area of the smaller polygon is 24cm2. What is the area of the larger polygon?

19. Three trapeziums are similar. The area of first trapeziums is 4 times that of the second and 5 times that of third. Determine the ratios of the perimeters and the corresponding side lengths of all the trapeziums.

20. Rectangle ABCD is similar to rectangle PQRS. Given that AB=14cm, BC=8cm and PQ=21 cm, calculate the length of QR.

21. A football field measures 100 m by 72 m. A school marks a football field similar in shape to a full size football field but only 30 m long. What is its width?

22. A graph is plotted to show relation between weekly growth rate and amount of light received by the plant.

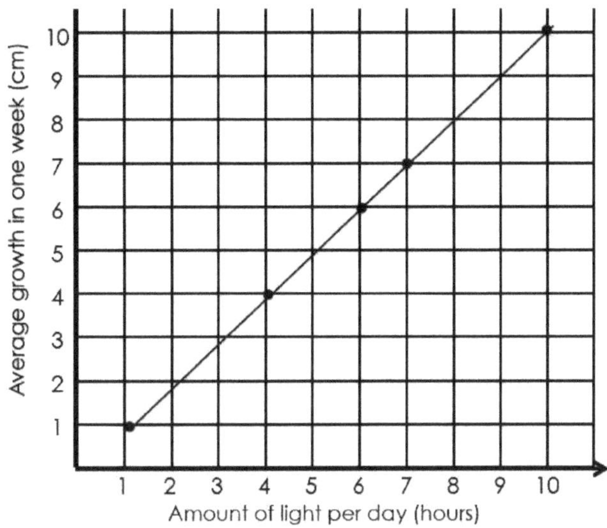

Find out the linear relation in between tow variables on the growth pattern. [Example 4 hours exposure = 4 cm growth per week.]

23. Estimate the part of each of the following grids which is shaded.

a.
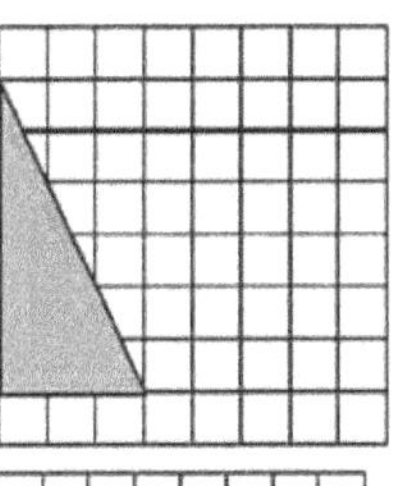

d.
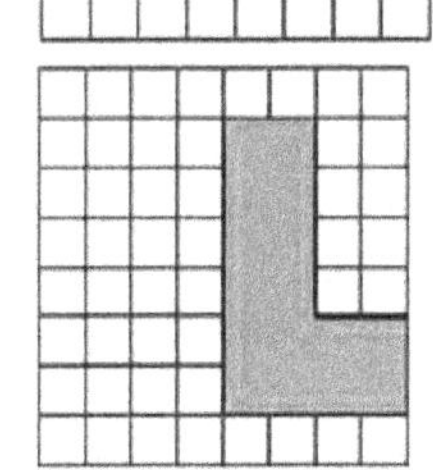

b.
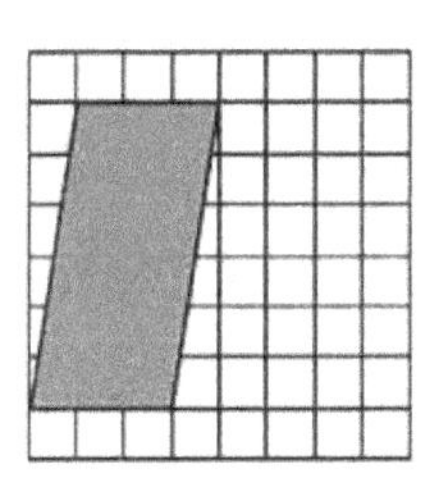

e.
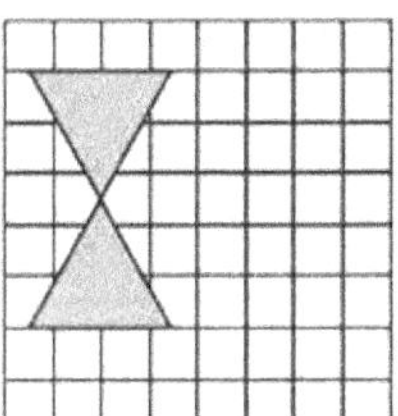

c.
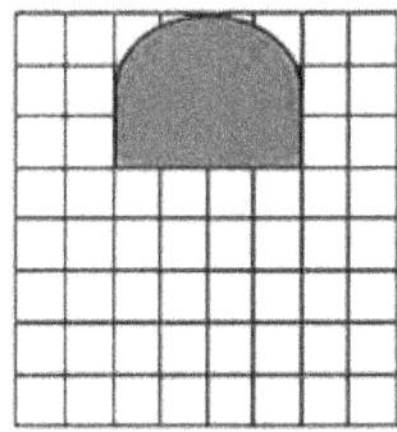

f.
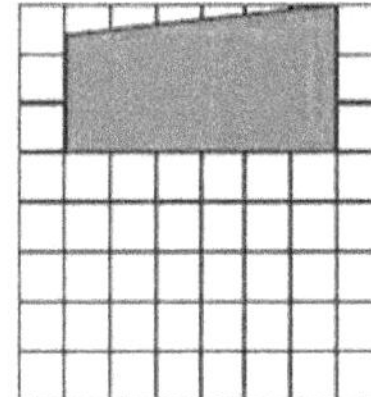

24. Cistern A fills up a water tank in 40 minutes. Cistern B fills up the same water tank in 1 h 20 minutes. If both the cisterns kept open then time taken by both the cisterns to fill up four such water tanks will be ………'

25. Tamanna took 4 days to finish her project works while working 5 hours a day. She can finish six such projects in …….. days while working three hours a day.

26. Arya observed that train A started crossing Train B after 3 minutes. Intermediate gap in between both the train was 1 km 80 m. Average seed of train B was 36 km/h. Find out Average speed of train A.

27: Find out a number A number between 2700 and 2800 when divided by 25 has a quotient that contains three odd digits and has no remainder.

28. A number p is in between 130 and 140 when divided by 12 has a quotient that contains the same two digits and has no remainder. Find out simplest value of p.

29. Sum of a natural number and its multiplicative inverse is equal to 8.125. Find out cube root of that number. Consider the natural number as a positive integer.

30. What least number should be subtracted from the product of three digit greatest number and four digit smallest numbers to obtain a multiple of 11?

31. Half of a bucket p, quarter of bucket q, one eleventh of bucket r holds equal volume of water. Compare volume of all these three buckets.

32. Roshanlal jogs at a speed of 18 km/h. Sohanlal accompanies him and moves 12 forward in 24 seconds. Find out the speed maintained by Sohanlal.

33. 29% of a natural number is equal to 101,001. Find out the number.

34. How many four digit numbers are there in all?

35. What least number should be subtracted from 43,86,035 to obtain a common multiple of 2 and 4?

Set 12

Find out surface area and volume of the following.

1: l = 12 cm, b = 8 cm, h = 6 cm   2: a cube of edge 12 cm

3: l = 20 cm; b = 18 cm; h = 10 cm;   4: a cube of edge 12.5 cm;

5: Three angles of a triangle are in the ratio of 2: 4: 7. Find out the angles.

6. Half of an angle is equal to quarter of its supplementary angle. Find out the angle.

7. Quarter of angle A, $3/5^{th}$ of angle B and $6/19^{th}$ of angle C jointly form a straight angle. Find out the angles.

8. Complementary of an angle is 39^0 32'. Find out the angle.

9. Angle A and B of a triangle jointly forms a right angle. Find out the third angle.

10. What fraction of all the natural numbers from 1 to 600 are common multiples of 30, 15 and 60?

11: What is the surface area of a utility cabinet that is 60 cm long, 46 cm wide, and 32 cm high?

12. Half of a cubical water tank of edge 1.5 m is filled with water. calculate total volume of water present in the tank. A cistern throws 200 cm^3 water in a second. Calculate total time to be taken by that cistern to fill up remaining parts of the tank.

13. What is the difference between the surface area of a cube that is 30 cm on an edge and a rectangular prism that is 40 cm long, 20 cm wide, and 10 cm high?

14. Quarter of a water tank is filled up by a cistern in 20 minutes. One fifth of another water tank is filled up by that cistern in 15 minutes. Calculate total time to be taken by that cistern to fill up both the water tanks completely.

15. Sonali and Monali jointly works to finish an assignment in 12 days. Monali alone can finish it in 18 days. Sonali alone can finish it in …. days.

16. What fraction of numbers from 1 to 100 are divisible by 5?

17: While moving from city to village Pallavi travelled half of total distance by bus, half of rest of the distance by auto, half of the remaining distance by city drive and remaining 870 m by walking. Calculate total distance travelled by her.

18. Anand kumar is 28 cm taller than Rikin and 9 cm shorter than Neha. Height of Neha is 14 cm less than her sister Sneha. Sneha recorded her height 21 cm less than 2 m. Find out height of all the fellow partners of the team.

19. Half of p, $3/5^{th}$ of q, $4/7^{th}$ of r, $7/9^{th}$ of s are equal to each other. Find out simplest ratio of p, q and r. Also find out simplest value of $(p^2 \ q^2 + r^2)$ and $2(pq + qr + rq)$

20. Smallest six digit number which is divisible by 9 leaving remainder 7 exceeds smallest six digit number by ....

21. $(1+ 2 + 3 + ...6000) \times 3,000 \times 125 \times 8 = 54,009 \times 10^{p}$; here p = ...

22. Quarter of a number exceeds product of greatest four digit number and smallest four digit number by 201. Find out the number.

23. Total distance travelled by Nikhil in 100 minutes is equal to 300 m. Find out total time to be taken by him to cover 54 km of distance.

24. Namrata, Sohanlal and Vineet preferred working together to finish a work in 4 days. They work with equal capacity. Find out time taken by Namrata alone to complete the same work.

25. How many three digit even numbers are there in all?

26. If 11 X 11 = 121; 111 X 111 = 12321; then 11,111 X 11,111 = ...

27. Complete the following number pattern: 1,   1,   2, ..., ..., 8, ...

28. P = 109 X 909 X 1009 X 3909 X 59899. If we write value of P in standard form then digit at ones place will be ....

29. If $(3 + 5 + 1) = 3 \times 3 = 9$; $(5 + 1 + 3 + 7) = 16$ then $(9 + 11 + 5 + 3 + 7 + 1) = $ ....

30. $7/11^{th}$ of $11/19^{th}$ of 38,57,095 = ...

Set 13

Calculate volume of the following in unit cube.

1. 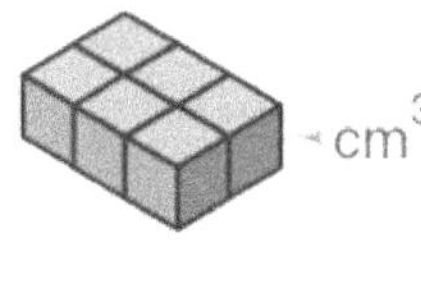 ‑ cm^3

2. 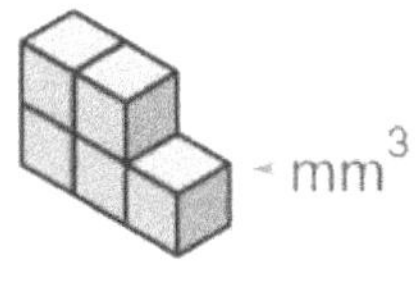 ‑ mm^3

3. 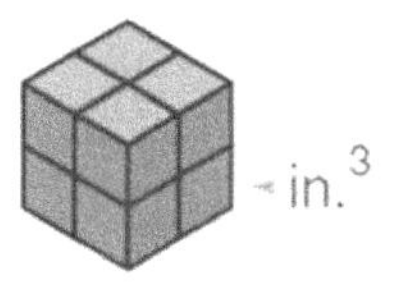 ‑ in.^{3}

4. 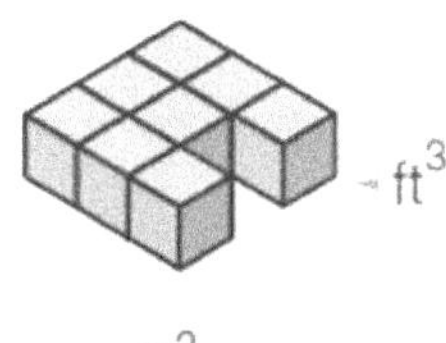 ‑ ft^3

___ cm^3 ___ mm^3 ___ in.^{3} ___ ft^3

5. 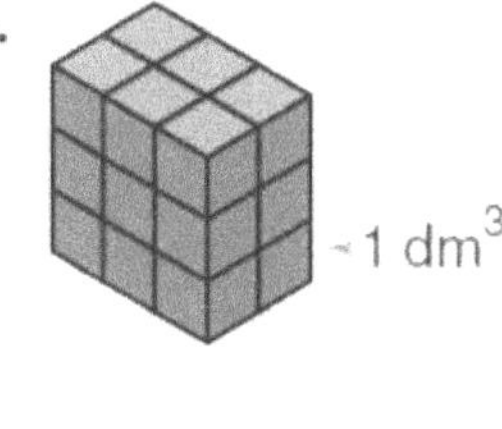 ‑ 1 dm^3

6. 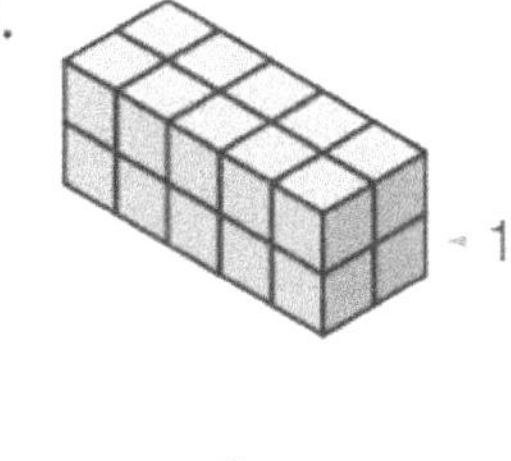 ‑ 1 ft^3

7. 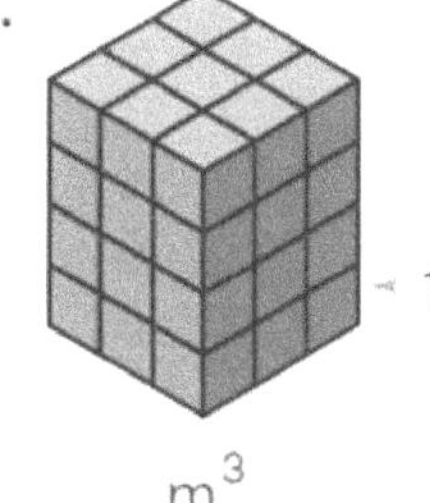 ‑ 1 m^3

8. 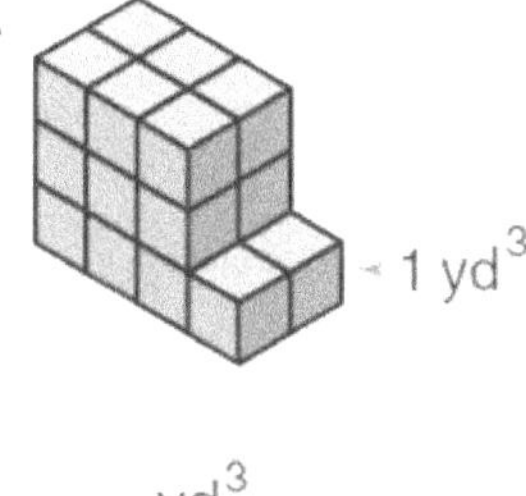 ‑ 1 yd^3

___ dm^3 ___ ft^3 ___ m^3 ___ yd^3

9: How many square centimeters of cardboard were used to make a cubical carton that is 3.5 cm on each edge?

10. 20% of tank A, 30% of tank B and 50% of tank C are equal to each other in terms of volume. Total capacity of all the three tanks is 4,000 m^3. Find out individual volume of the tanks.

11. Volume of a cubical tank is 1331 m^2. Find out edge of this water tank. Also find out area of the bottom.

Work out best estimation

12. crayon box   a. 500 m^3 b. 500 dm^3 c. 500 cm^3

13. tissue box   a. 90 in.^{3} b. 90 ft^3 c. 90 yd^3

14. CD   a. 140 mm^3 b. 140 cm^3 c. 140 m^3

15. Tina made a design by pasting an isosceles right triangle in the center of a square of side 10 cm. If the length of each perpendicular side of the triangle is 5.2 cm, what is the area of the square that is still visible?

16. A special pop-up birthday card has a mass of 12.5 g. The card store sells these cards in a pack that weighs about 2.5 kg. About how many pop-up cards are in each pack?

17. A birdfeeder is 36 cm by 30 cm by 12 cm. A sack of birdseed has a volume of 14 dm3. Is this enough birdseed to fill the feeder? If there exists any difference then calculate such difference.

18. Nikita took a test paper having 45 questions. She had 21 answers correct. What is the ratio of the number of correct answers to the number of incorrect answers?

19. What percent of greatest five digit number is equal to 1250?

20. A natural number is equal to 1002 greater than third multiple of the greatest three digit number?

21. Is it possible to shade a 10 X 10 grid so that it is 15% blue, 75% red, and 20% green?

22. After selling 11 cards a shopkeeper gained an amount equal to selling price of one card. Find out total gain percentage of the shopkeeper.

23. Half of A, quarter of B, one sixth of C are equal to each other. Find out simplest value of the following:

$$\left(\frac{1}{A} + \frac{1}{B} + \frac{1}{C}\right) X (2A + 3B + 4C)$$

24. What least number should be subtracted from four digit greatest number and five digit smallest number to find out a common dividend which can be divided by 2, 3, 4 and 11 leaving remainder 1 in each case?

Simplify the following:

25. $(1 + 2 + \ldots\ldots 3{,}000) X 1{,}500 \div 3{,}001$

26. 2001 times 5 + 4,002 times 6 + 8,004 times 7 = $\ldots\ldots$ X 2001

Set 14

1. Three seventh of a natural number exceeds third multiple of seven digit number by 3,003. Find out the number.

2. Work out the numerical value of a in the following to make the following equations true.

A. $\frac{3}{4} + \left(\frac{1}{2} + \frac{3}{5}\right) = \left(\frac{3}{4} + \frac{1}{2}\right) + a$ 　　　B. $\frac{5}{9} + \left(a + \frac{2}{3}\right) = \left(\frac{5}{9} + \frac{1}{6}\right) + \frac{2}{3}$

C. $\frac{1}{4} \times \left(a + \frac{1}{5}\right) = \left(\frac{1}{4} \times \frac{1}{3}\right) + \left(\frac{1}{4} \times \frac{1}{5}\right)$

3. $(A + B) = 109$; $(B + C) = 207$; $(C + D) = 309$; $(D + A) = 403$; Find out simplest value of $(A + B + C + D)$.

4. 25% of a natural number exceeds 11,001 by 3001. Find out the number.

5. What fraction of 125,125,125 is equal to 125?

6. A passenger train takes 2 minutes and 45 seconds to cross a tunnel of length 1 km 300 m. Average speed of that train is 72 km/h. Find length of that train.

7. Represent the following by using percentage.

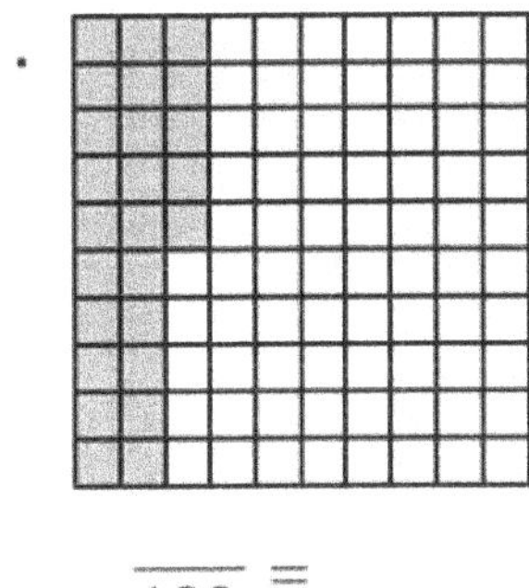 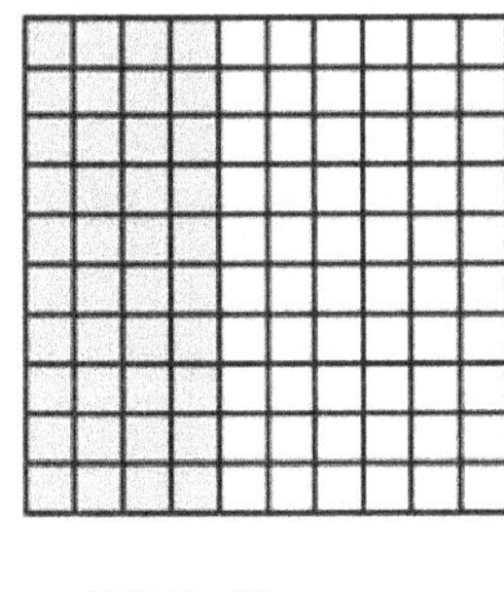 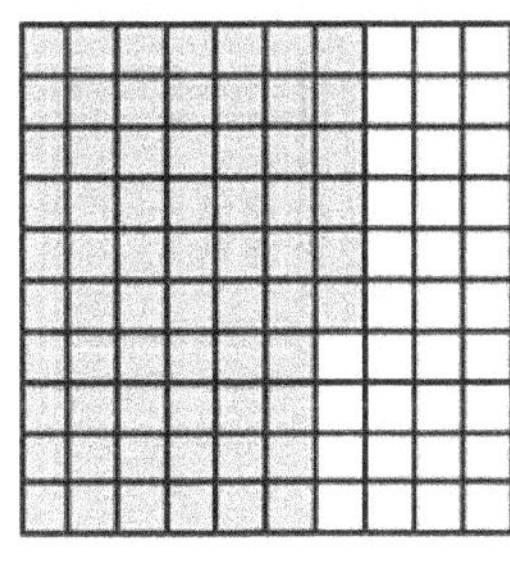

$\overline{100} = \underline{\quad}$ 　　　　　$\overline{100} = \underline{\quad}$ 　　　　　$\overline{100} = \underline{\quad}$

8. What percentage of 125,125 is equal to 1001?

9. Is there any pair of number having LCM 2003 and HCF 198?

10. How many four digit numbers are there in all?

11. Sum of length and breadth of a rectangle is equal 25 cm. Area of that rectangle is equal to 154 sq. cm. Find out length and breadth of that rectangle.

12. Sum of an angle and one fifth of its complementary angle is equal to 54^0. Find out supplementary of that angle.

13. How many seven digit numbers are there in all?

14. What least number should be subtracted from product of greatest and smallest number of five digits to obtain a dividend which can be divided individually by 4, 6, 12 and 18 leaving remainder 3 in each case?

15: Nancy bought a bag of red, white, and blue balloons for the birthday party. There were total number of 49 balloons in the bag. If there are 2 times as many red as blue and half as many white as blue baloons, how many of each color balloon are there in the bag?

16. There are 12 mail carriers in Tundon Town. Monday, they delivered 24,780 letters. Letters being delivered on Tuesday was 36,720. Each carrier delivered the same number of letters. How many letters did each carrier deliver in two days?

17. Three fourth of a number exceeds third multiple of smallest five digit number by 309. Find out the number.

18. ($1/5^{th}$ of 5,005 + $1/6^{th}$ f 6,006 + $1/7^{th}$ of 7,007) $\div$ 1,001 = ...

19. What fraction of all the natural numbers starting from 500 are multiples of 25?

20. Which natural number of six digits will be the smallest multiple of 9?

21. (1.001 X 0.001 X 0.01 X 12,904) X 10^5 = ...

22. Half of $1/7^{th}$ of 14,28,510 = ...

23. "Sum of three interior angle of a triangle is equal to 180^0. First angle is complementary to the second angle." If this statement is true then what will be the magnitude of the third angle of that triangle?

24. 30% of a number exceeds 300 by 60. Find out the number.

Set 15

1: Find out smallest four digit number which is divisible by 4, 5, 6 and 7 leaving remainder 3 in each case.

2. In her coin book, Sylvia wants to arrange 18 French coins and 24 Spanish coins and 36 Asian coins in equal rows on the page. What is the greatest number of Spanish, French or Asian coins she can arrange in each row? How many rows will she have in this way?

3. What least number should be subtracted from greatest six digit number to obtain a common multiple of 3, 6, 9 and 18?

4. Provide missing values.

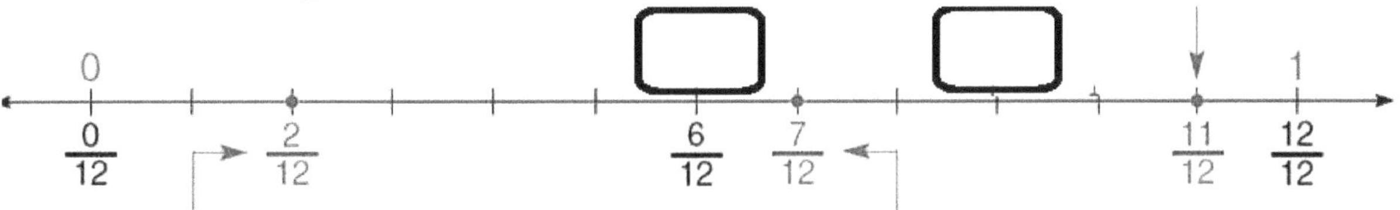

5. Find out value of n in the following.

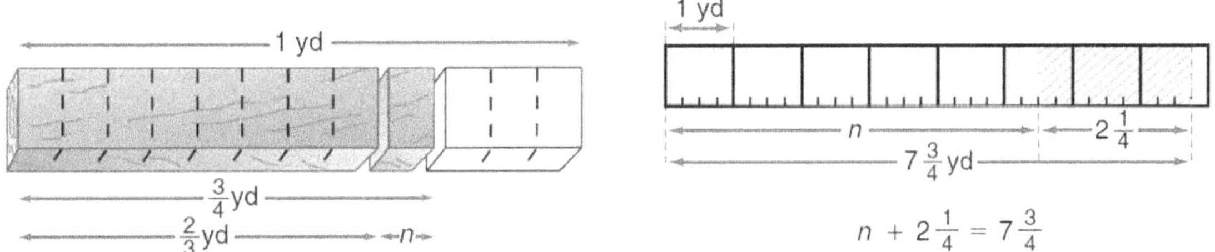

6. Half of $1/11^{th}$ of a natural number is equal to 10,20,300. Find out the number. Also find out sixth multiple of that number.

7. 20% f 70% of a natural number exceeds 14th multiple of smallest number of four digits by 56. Find out the number.

8. What least number should be subtracted from greatest number of six digits to obtain a number which can be divided by 6, 12 and 18 leaving remainder 5 in each case?

9. Sonalika prepares three toys in 3 days while working 3 hours a day. Find out number of days needed to 12 toys while working 4 hours a day.

10. Write when the fractional part of the difference of two mixed numbers is equal to zero; also write when the whole-number part of the difference is equal to zero. Use models to explain your answers.

11. What digit will be there in the product of greatest and smallest number of five digits?

12. Train A moves 20 m in 1 second and train B covers 36 km in 1 hour. They started moving towards each other through up and down tracks respectively. When there was a gap of 108 km a bird started flying to and fro in between both the engines. The bird continued flying until and unless both the engines started crossing each other. The bird covers 54 km in 1 hour. Calculate total time taken by the bird to fly to and fro in between both the engines, also find out total distance travelled by the bird while flying so.

13. What fraction of all the natural numbers starting from 1 to 1000 are multiples of 20?

14. Is there any pair of natural number having LCM 1331 and HCF 121?

15. Three ringing bells toll together at an interval of 3 seconds, 5 seconds and 8 seconds. How many times do all these bells toll together in a span of a couple of hour?

16. 37th of $5/9^{th}$ of a natural number is equal to 125,125,075. Find out the number.

Combination Worksheets

Worksheet 1

Write the place of the underlined digit. Then write its value.

1. 2242　　　　　2. 63,666　　　　　3. 199,999　　　　　4. 880,888

Place a comma where needed in each. Then write the period name for the underlined digit.

5. 3 4 2 5 _9　　　　　6. 1 6 4 3 2　　　　　7. 2 0 0 0 6 0　　　　　8. 8 0 5 0 2 7

Write the number in standard form.

9. forty-five thousand, seven hundred sixty-two 10. five thousand, six

11. nine hundred thousand, seven　　　　　12. ten thousand, nineteen

Write the word name for each number.

13. 217,046　　　14. 737,008　　　15. 16,231,075　　　16. 12,923,780

Round to the nearest hundred.

13. 158　　14. 426　　15. 375　　16. 896　　17. 719　　18. 950

19. 1047　　20. 3888　　21. 5942　　22. 6891　　23. 3098　　24. 8762

25. 37,405　26. 62,345　27. 88,088　28. 65,097　29. 58,706　30. 66,636

Round to the nearest thousand.

31. 9155　　32. 7983　　33. 4550　　34. 6237　　35. 8396

36. 33,888　37. 15,942　38. 93,192　39. 87,983　40. 46,237

41. 326,150 42. 145,706 43. 357,029 44. 563,498 45. 807,476

46. 821,593 47. 450,513 48. 435,127 49. 205,120 50. 761,604

51. Find the six digit greatest multiple of 8.

52. Write in standard form: $2{,}000{,}000 + 3 \times 10^5 + 400{,}000 + 3 \text{ tens} + 15 \text{ tenths} + 4$

Worksheet 2

1. If 10 is added to a number it becomes the 10th multiple of 10100. Find the number.

2. Niharika wants a pencil. It costs Rs. 10. She gives nine one rupee coin, one-half rupee coin and one-quarter rupee coin. Is it enough?

3. Comlete the following number patterns:

Look at the patterns and complete them.

3, 6, 9, 12 ___,___,____.   2, 4, 6,___,___,____.

8, 16, 24, 32,___,___,____.   4, 8, 12, 16, ___,___,____.

5, 10, 15,___,___,____.   30, 60, 90,___,___,____.

A1, B2, C3, D4,___,___,____.   12A, 13B, 14C,___,___,____.

51, 56, 61, 66, ,___,___,____.   1, 2, 3, 4, 5 ,___,___,____.

10, 20, 30,___,___,____.   1, 3, 6, 10, 15, ___,___,____.

2, 4, 8, 16, 32,___,___,____.   12, 24, 36, 48, ___,___,____.

4. If 11 X 11 = 121 and 111 X 111 = 12321 then 1111 X 1111 = ____________________.

5. Rajat can finish half of a project in 12 days and Meena alone can finish quarter of the same project in 6 days. They jointly can finish entire project in _____ days.

6. Form the greatest and smallest 4 digit number by using digits 8,4,0 and 3. Also find their difference.

7. Find the perimeter of a rectangle having length 32 cm and breadth 20 cm.

8. Total cost of 3 pens and 2 pencils is Rs 25. In another combination total cost of 2 pens and 3 pencils is Rs 20.

    a. Find the total cost of 2 pens and 2 pencils.

    b. Also find the total cost of 5 pens and 4 pencils.

    c. Find the cost of 1 pen.

   d. Find the cost of 1 pencil.

9. What fraction of the greatest number of 4 digits is equal to 1111?

10: Find the greatest and smallest number of four digits having different digits at their respective places.

11: ______ million is the 1000th multiple of the greatest even number of 5 digit.

12: $\frac{11}{29}$ of $\frac{29}{709}$ of $\frac{1418}{1,001}$ of $\frac{7,007}{12100}$ = ________

13: 30th multiple of 11 is ______ more than 6th multiple of 50.

14: _____ is the smallest number to be subtracted from 1009 to make it a multiple of 6.

15: $1,000^{th}$ multiple of the product of all the factors of 29 is ______ less than the 6th multiple of 5,000.

16: Complete the following to obtain values in the form of product of prime factors:

   a. 1410 = ______ X___;

   b. 1331 = __________________.

   c. 169 = __________________.

   d. $1/10^{th}$ of $9/17^{th}$ of 5100 = ________________.

   e. 21 hundredths added to 11 tenths = ______________.

   f. $\left(\frac{84}{0.004}\right)$ = ________________;

   g. 363 = __________ X __________ ;

   h. 3,000 = 2 X 2 X 2 X ______________

   i. 729 = __ X __X___ X ___X___;

   j. __________ = 89 X 11

   k. 9th multiple of 11 is ________ multiple of 9.

   l. By subtracting __we obtain 3rd multiple of 13 from the 4th multiple of 10.

17: Some of the statements regarding prime and composite numbers are given below.

     I :   1 is not a prime or composite number.

     II :   Two is the only even prime number.

     III: All odd numbers are not prime.

     IV: All composite numbers can be written as product of prime numbers.

     V: 101 has only two factors 1 and the number itself. That is why it is a prime number

Which of the above statements are true?

A: Only I   B: All   C: I, II and III   D: Only II, III and IV

18: Sum total of place values of 6 in the following set of numbers = __ .

     26,754,   64,543   23,362

     A: 66,600   B: 66,060   C: 60,606   D: 16,000

19: What least number should be subtracted from the five digit greatest even number to make it divisible by 11?

20: _____ can be added to the greatest five digit multiple of 5 to make it divisible by 6.

21: Complete the following:

    a. (0.5 + 0.5 + 0.5 ….. 500 times) − (0.25 + 0.25 + 0.25 + ….. 1000 times) = _________.

    b. Half of 16 + quarter of 20 + one seventh of 49 = _________.

    c. ______ is the greatest prime number of two digits which is in the ______ position if we write all the prime numbers starting from the smallest one.

    d. Length of the paper strip made by joining 16 square sized paers of area 16 sq. cm each is equal to _____ cm.

    e. __________ is the greatest five digit multiple of six.

    f. Sum total of greatest five digit multiple and dmallest four digit multiple of 2

=

    g. Anamika can finish $1/20^{th}$ of her project works in 30 minutes. She can finish the entire project in _____ days while working 5 hours a day.

22: Every cubic millimeter of human blood contains near about about 7500 white blood cells. A count less than 1500 above this number is still considered healthy. Is a white cell count of a person reaching 8750 considered healthy?

23: Earth's total surface area is about $19,956 \times 10^{4}$ square miles. Approximately $139,692 \times 10^{3}$ square miles of the Earth surface are covered with water. About how much of Earth's surface is covered by land? Estimate your finding to the nearest million?

24: 46th multiple of 1/92 of 121,121 = __________________.

25: 125 X 8 = 1,000 and 40 X 25 = 1,000. Now complete the following expressions:

    a) $1005 \times 125 \times 100 \times 8 = 1.005 \times 10^{n}$. Find the value of n.
    b) 40 X 9003 X 8 = 125 X 9003 X _______.
    c) $21021 \times 25 \times 125 \times$ ___ $\times 40 = 21.021 \times 10^{9}$;

26:Each necklace uses 72 cm of wire. Will a 5000 cm roll of wire be enough to make 75 necklaces? If not, how much more wire will be needed?

27: Palady rented a shop at Town Hall Market. It sold 18 pairs of earrings at Rs. 5,500 each and 8 belts at Rs 350.75 each. How much money did the shopkeeper collect from the sales?

28: It is observed by Rikin that on Saturday morning there were 1,205 people at the Shopping Mall Market. There was double that number in the afternoon. The number was three times during evening time How many people came to the Market on Saturday?

29: Fancy belts are made of braided cords. Each belt uses 96 cm. of cord. Will a 12 m roll of cord be enough to make a dozen belts?

30: Last year Tuna sold 204 necklaces which was 15 more than her sale of two years back. This year she sold twice that number. How many necklaces did Kelly sell in the past three years?

31: A rural village's population is between 800 and 1000. The sum of the digits in its population is 21, and the digits in the ones and the hundreds places are the same. What might be the population of the village?

32: Tamanna has 10 pieces of gum to share with her friends. There wasn't enough gum for all her friends, so she went to the store and got 70 pieces of strawberry gum and 12 packs each containing10 pieces of bubble gum. How many pieces of gum does Adrianna have now?

33: Chintu started back counting by 5 starting from 200. He stopped after counting for 19 times. Find the value that he has obtained at this step.

34: Tokino is painting a portrait of her best friend, Mona. To make it easier, she divides half of the portrait into 6 equal parts. What fraction represents each part of the portrait?

Worksheet 3

1. Find areas enclosed by the following figures:

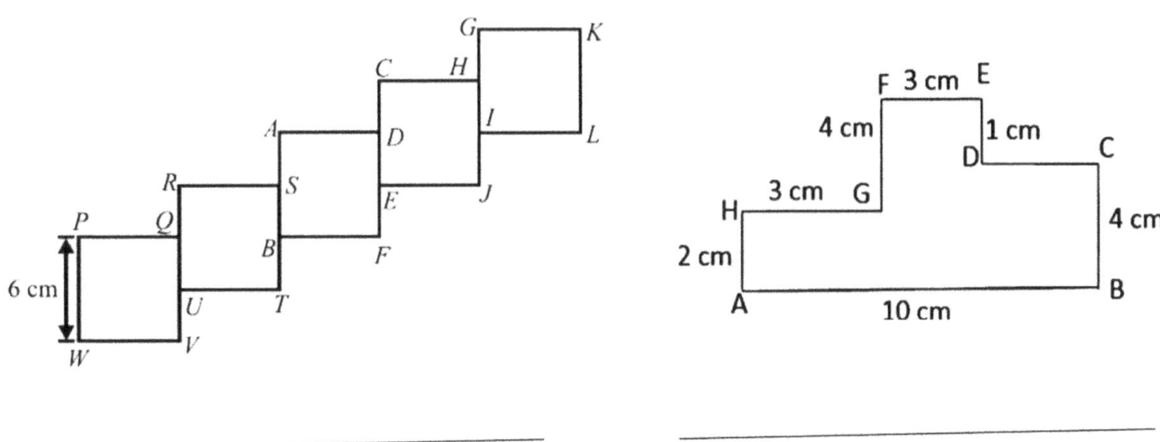

2. Harpreet observed that a wall mount clock strikes 4 bells at 4 O'Clock in 4 seconds. It will strike 10 bells at 10 O'Clock in _____ seconds.

3. Bandarnayake observed that a Goods Train covered a distance of 100 m in ten seconds. Another Mail train covers 72 km in one hour. Compare speed of both the train.

4. Mr. Bandarnayake finishes his journey of 120 km in 2 and half hours. While moving with same speed he has visited his native place and it took him 45 minutes to drive to and fro his native place from his home of countryside. Find the distance of his native place from the countryside.

5. What least number must be subtracted from a seven digit greatest number to make the number divisible by 11?

6. Dhanu has the longest jump of 3 metres 40 cm. Gurjeet is second. His jump is 20 cm less than Dhanu's. Gopi comes third.

    His jump is only 5 cm less than Gurjeet's jump.

    How long are Gurjeet's and Gopi's jumps?

    Try and see how far you can jump.

    How far can you throw a ball? _____________ metres.

    Look for a big ball, like a football or volleyball. How far can you kick it? _________

    CONVERSION

    4 m 55 cm = ______ cm   7 m 6 cm = ______ cm   8 m 89 cm = ______ cm

    7 m 45 cm = ______ cm   3 m 16 cm = ______ cm   18 m 8 cm = ______ cm

    8 km 45 m = ____ km   5 km 520 m = ______ km   44 km 660 m = ____ km

    18 km 425 m = ____ km   5 km 50 m = ______ km   23 km 166 m = ____ km

7. Observe the table depicted below and aanswer questions as follows: ---

Sports	World Record	Indian Record
High Jump (Men)	Javier S. (2m 45 cm)	Chandra Pal (2m 17 cm
Long Jump (Men)	Mike P. (8m 95 cm)	Amrit Pal (8m 8 cm)
High Jump (Women)	Stefka K. (2m 9 cm)	Bobby A. (1m 91 cm)
Long Jump (Women)	Galina C. (7m 52 cm)	Anju G. (6m 83 cm)

    A. How many centimetres more should Chandra Pal jump to equal the Men'sWorld Record for high jump?

B. How many centimetres higher should Bobby A. jump to reach 2 metres?

    Remember that 1m= 100 cm;

    Half metre = ______ cm; one and half metre = ______;

    C. Galina's long jump is nearly

    a) 7 metres   b) 7 and a half metres   c) 8 metres

D. Look at the Women's World Records. What is the difference between the longest jump and the highest jump?

E. If Mike P. could jump _______ centimetres longer, his jump would be full 9 metres.

F. Whose high jump is very close to two and half metres?

a) Stefka K.   b) Chandra Pal   c) Javier S.   d) Bobby A.

9: Make 3 different 3 digit numbers using 1, 9 and 8, where each digit can be used only once. Check which of these numbers are divisible by 9.

10: Which numbers among 2, 3, 5, 6, 9 divides 12345 exactly? Write 12345 in reverse order and test now which numbers divide it exactly?

11: Write different 2 digit numbers using digits 3, 4 and 5. Check whether these numbers are divisible by 2, 3, 5, 6 and 9?

12: Write the smallest digit and the greatest possible digit in the blank space of each of the following numbers so that the number formed are divisible by 3.

    i. __ 6724   ii. 4765__ 2   iii. 7221__ 5

13: Find the smallest number that must be added to 123, so that it becomes exactly divisible by 5?

14: Find the smallest number that has to be subtracted from 256, so that it becomes exactly divisible by 10?

15: Prasad and Raju met in the market on 1st of this month. Prasad goes to the market every 3rd day and Raju goes every 4th day. On what day of the month will they meet again?

16: During an experiment Dana recorded the following temperatures: 22°C, 12°C, 15°C, 5°C, 8°C. If this pattern continues, predict the tenth temperature in the series.

17: Scientists built earthquake stations at different elevations. One station is 75 m above sea level, and a second is 35 m below sea level. What is the difference in height between the two stations?

18: A diamond-mine entrance begins at 75 ft above sea level. Workers discover diamonds 48 ft below sea level. How deep is the mine at that point?

19: A parachutist opens her parachute at an altitude of 5000 ft. Her change in altitude is 25 ft per second.

    a. Write an equation to find her altitude h at a time after she opens her parachute.

    b. How far, written as an integer, has she descended in 12 seconds?

    c. What is her altitude 12 seconds after she opens her parachute?

20. How many three digit numbers can be made by using three different digit without repeating any of them? Arrange them in ascending rder.

21. Three interior angles of a triange are such that two times of third angle and three times of second angle are equal to the first angle. Find out the angles.

22. What least number should be subtracted from five digit greatest number to make it exactly divisible by 5?

23. A wall mount clock takes three secnds to strike three bells. It will strike 11 bells in ……….. seconds.

24. How many line segments can be drawn passing through a given point?

25. Find out a smallest five digit number divisible by 3.

26. Ravi can do half of a work alone in 12 days, Munish can do quarter of the same work in 18 days and Roushan can complete one tenth of the work in 2 days. If they all join hands to complete the same work then by what time the entire work will be finished?

Worksheet 4

1. Find the equivalent number in standard form:

$$(2 \times 100) + \left(30\,X\,\frac{1}{10}\right) + \left(4\,X\,\frac{1}{10}\right) + \left(22\,X\,\frac{1}{100}\right) + \left(121\,X\,\frac{1}{1000}\right)$$

2. How many different angles are formed? Write names of each angle.

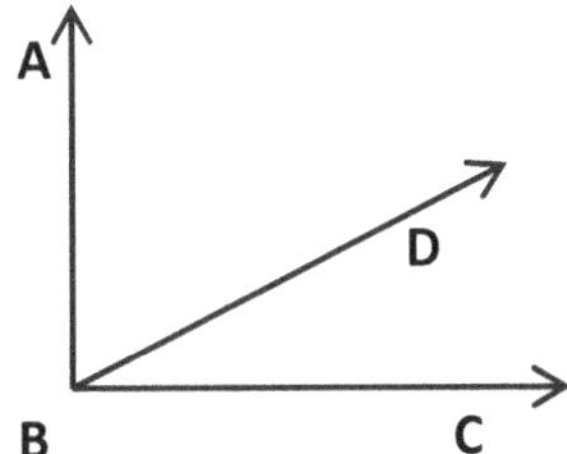

3. If two lines intersect each other at a definite point then how many pairs of vertically opposite angles are formed?

4. Which of the following is not a property of rectangles?

   a. Opposite sides are parallel to each other.
   b. Opposite angles are supplementary to each other.
   c. All the interior angles are right angles.
   d. Pair of diagonals intersects each other at right angle.
   e. Sum total of all the interior angles is equal to two straight angles.
   f. Two greatest possible triangles can be adjusted inside it without overlapping.
   g. It is a special type of parallelogram.

    h. This figure cannot be defined as a square.

5. Mr Ravikumar can paint a wall in 6 days and his counterpart can paint it in 12 days. Both of them jointly can paint it in _________ days.

6. The measure of an angle is 54^0. What is the measure of its complement?

7. Write T for true or F for false for the following statements.

    a. There are eight prime numbers in between 1 and 20.

    b. All prime numbers has only one factor.

    c. All composite numbers has more than two factors.

    d. 69 is a multiple of 1, 3 and 23.

    e. There is only one prime number in between 90 and 100.

    f. Sum total of 21 hundredths and 543 thousandths is greater than 1.

    g. All natural numbers are not composite numbers.

    h. Any number divisible by 5 should have digit 0 or 5 at its one's place.

    i. Any number divisible by 8 is also divisible separately by all the other factors of 8, 4 and 2.

8. Rikin pointed out a mistake in the representation of a greatest five digit number divisible by 11 submitted by his friend Mike and corrected the mistake by reducing the digit at one's place by 4. What was the result submitted by Mike?

9. Ramantha observed that sum total of three consecutive prime number is 15. Sum total of the first and last prime number is half of the second one. Find all the prime numbers.

10. Aman and Natalia went on completing their projects jointly in 16 days. If Aman alone could do it in 32 days then Natalia alone could do it in ______ days.

11. Bishan Singh three cu. m. earth in a day by working 8 hours a day. An assignment was issued to him to dig a chamber of dimension 6 m X 10 m X 10 m by working

10 hours a day at the time of emergency. Bishan Singh could complete his assignment in _______ days.

12. Find the least number which can divide 126, 25,200 and 504,000 exactly without leaving any remainder.

13. Find the least numbers to be subtracted from each of the following numbers to make them all divisible by 11:

992, 9994, 99999, 9090907, 880,880,880

14. Arrange the following in ascending order:

20% of 12, 30 % of 32 , one sixth of 18.18, three seventh of 49.49

15. There exists some similarity between regular pentagon and regular hexagon. Identify the point which cannot signify their similarities.
    a. Sum total of all the exterior angles of both the polygon is equal to a complete angle.
    b. Interior angle of the hexagon is 36^0 more than that of the pentagon.
    c. Number of diagonals in pentagon is 5 and number such diagonals in hexagon is 9.
    d. Three non- overlapping triangles can be accommodated in pentagon and four such triangles can be accommodated in hexagon.
16. Place a suitable digit at the place marked as * to make the given numbers divisible by both 3 and 9.

126*9, 1322*76, 206,54*,121*32

17. Which greatest three digit number is divisible exactly by 4?

18. Roshanlal divided a rectangle in eight equal parts and observed that if such square sized cut pieces are arranged serially side by side then a rectangle of perimeter 36 cm is obtained. Find the dimension of the original rectangle.

19. When 0.02968 is divided by 0.008, what will be the quotient?

20. If we multiply a fraction by itself and divide the product by its reciprocal, the fraction thus obtained is $18\frac{26}{27}$. What is the original fraction?

21. A triangle having any two sides equal to each other should have _______ angles equal to each other. The unequal side will be _____________ to the unequal angle.

22. Mohanlal painted $1/20^{th}$ of a wall in 4 days. He will complete his works in _____ days.

23. A flower garden is 22.50 m long. Sheela wants to make a border along one side using bricks that are 0.25 m long. How many bricks will be needed?

24. What least number should be added to increase the digit of thousands place of 121,032 to obtain a common multiple of 3 and 9?

Worksheet 5

1. I obtained 60 marks out of 75 marks. What is the percentage of my marks?

2. Saima spent Rs 300 out of Rs 500. Find percentage of her expenditure.

3. There were 8500 voters in a village. 34% did not cast their votes. Find the number of voters who cast their votes.

4. The population of a village is 15000. If the population increases by 5% in a year, find the population after one year.

5. Rahila pays 5% of her salary in charity in a month. If she pays Rs 200, find her monthly salary.

6. The 18% of the distance between two cities is 36 km. Find the distance between two cities.

7. Naeem's monthly income is Rs 8000 and he spends Rs 6000 per month. Find the percentage of his expenditure.

8. On a rainy day 600 students out of 750 were present in a school. What percentage of the students was absent?

9. How many diagonals are there in a hexagon?

10. Simplify: $\left(1 + \frac{1}{100}\right) \times \left(1 - \frac{91}{101}\right) \times \left(1 + \frac{1}{1000}\right) \times \left(1 - \frac{901}{1001}\right) \times 1313 = $ _____ X 0.01

11. What least number should be subtracted from 101,112 to make the number exactly divisible by 101?

12. A seven digit number is represented as follows:

H Th	T Th	Th	H	T	O
3	2	6	8	___	___

Statement: This number is the greatest possible multiple of 8 located in between 326,880 and 326,900. The number is also divisible by 2 and 4. The number is also divisible by 16.

Provide the maximum possible digits at tens and ones place to make the given statement true.

13. A craftsperson earns $ 3.03 per hor. He works 8 hours a day and five days a week. Find his earnings of 5 weeks duration.

14. 21% of 40% of 100100 = _______________ .

15: Observe the figure:

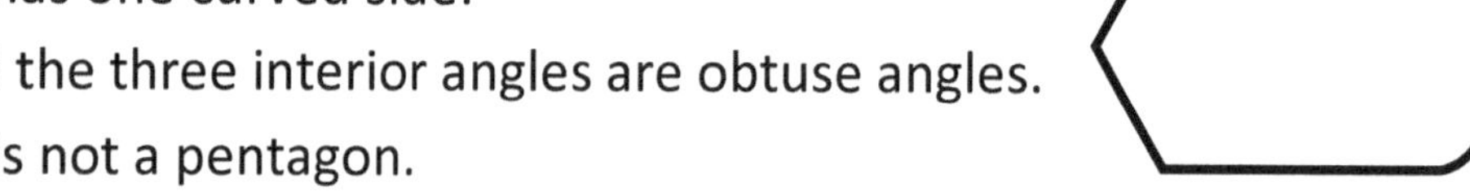

    a. It is not a polygon.

    b. It has one curved side.

    c. All the three interior angles are obtuse angles.

    d. It is not a pentagon.

    e. Which of the above statements are true?

        A: a and b   B: Only b   C: none   D: all

16. For which of the following conditions would you use a histogram to represent data?

  (i) The number of letters for different areas in a postman's bag.

  (ii) The height of competitors in an athletics meet.

  (iii) The number of cassettes produced by 5 companies.

  (iv) The number of passengers boarding trains from 7 a.m to 7 p.m at a station.

17. The following list records the shoppers who visited during the first hour in the morning.

W W W G B W W M G G M M W W W W

G B M W B G G M W W M M W W W

M W B W G M W W W W G W M M W

W M W G W M G W M M B G G W

Make a frequency distribution table using tally marks. Draw a bar graph to illustrate it.

18. How many five digit numbers are there in all?

19. What least number should be subtracted from six digit greatest number to make it divisible by 4?

20. Pallavi subtracted a smallest possible digit from thousands place of the give number 37,981 to make the number divisible by 3. Find out the value which was subtracted from the given number.

21. A container made of glass is partially filled with water. In the given diagram QR = 40 cm, UT = 20 cm, ST = 10 cm and VT = 8 cm. Find the volume of water that can be filled in it to make the container completely filled with water.

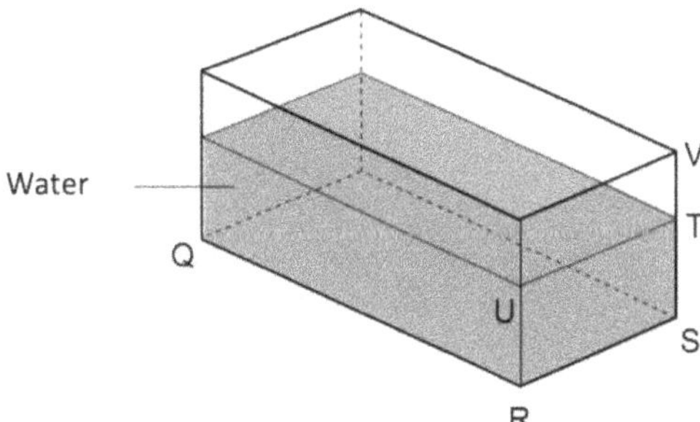

22. How many four digit even numbers are there in all?

23. What least number should be subtracted from 32,90,898 to obtain a common multiple of 3, 6 and 9?

24. For every 1^0 C increase of temperature there is a corresponding increase of 1.8^0 F. If temperature of a city is increased by 32^0 C, then calculate corresponding increase of termperature in ^{0} F.

Worksheet 6

1. Rohit had a candy bar divided into 16 equal parts. He gave 3 pieces to Kamalika and 2 pieces to Mohan. What fraction of Candy bar is left with him?
2. Mohan added 43 tens and 387 hundreds to get a five digit number which is ____________ less than the six digit smallest number.

3. How many faces are there in the following shape?

4. There are ______ curved face(s) and _____ flat faces in a solid cylinder.
5. Mohan reached his office by 15 minutes late. It was 11:28 A.M. What was his office time?
6. While calculating perimeter of her garden Ratna calculated the length and breadth of the garden. It was 1500 m long and 600 m wide. _____ times the sum total of length and _________ will be the perimeter of the garden. Find the perimeter in km.
7. For a punch bowl, Carin needs a block of ice with a volume of at least 125 cubic inches. She has a cube of ice that is five inches on each side. Write the volume of the cube using a base and exponents. Then write it in standard form. Is the block of ice big enough? Remember that volume is calculated by multiplying length times width times height.

8. Tickets to the school play cost Rs 300 for adults and Rs 200 for students. If 235 adults and 322 students attended the play, write an expression that shows the total amount of money made on ticket sales. Then simplify the expression.

9. During vacation you spent Rs 127 out of Rs 250. There was another 500 rupees note with you. Find the money left with you.

10. The Akshi Kaikyo suspension bridge in Japan has a span of 6,570 feet. The Humber suspension bridge in England has a span of 4,626 feet. How much longer is the Humber suspension bridge than the Akshi Kaikyo suspension bridge?

11. Julio increases the laps he runs by three laps each day. If he begins on Monday running 4 laps, how many laps will he run on Wednesday at his current rate?

12. Adam is starting a business to take people on hot-air balloon rides. He knows that to carry 2 people, the balloon must have a volume of about 60,000 cubic feet. For his business, he wants a balloon that will carry 4 people. He calculates that the balloon must have a volume of 120,000 cubic feet. Is his answer reasonable? Explain.

13. _________ is the only natural number having only one factor.

14. A ___________ has no end point, a _______ has only one end point and a ________ ___________ has two endpoints.

15. A circular wire is reshaped to form a square of 20 cm side. What was the circumference of that circle?

16. Find the difference of areas of two squares having sides 30 cm and 40 cm respectively.

17. A swimming pool measures 50 m by 20 m. The manager plans to construct a cemented road around the pool, which should measure 4 m wide. What is the area of the cemented road?

Worksheet 7

1. Observe the process of representing a factor tree.

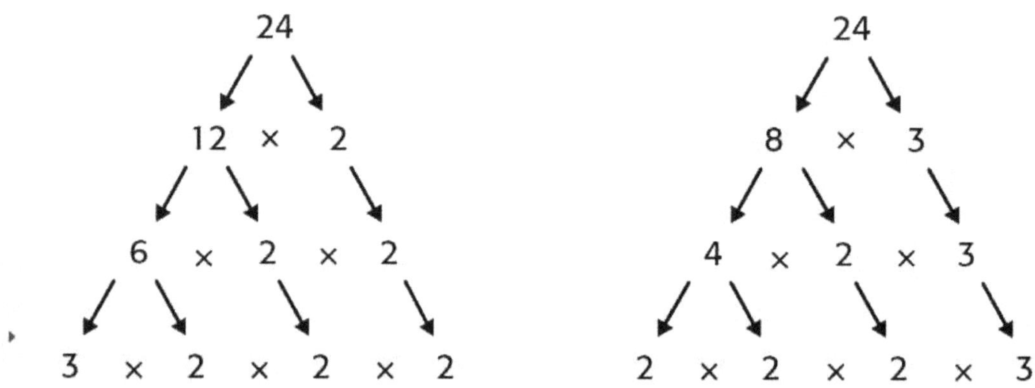

In the same way make a factor tree of number 72. Also write prime factorisation of the same. Is there any difference in two types of representations as displayed?

2. Rohit had a candy bar divided into 16 equal parts. He gave 3 pieces to Kamalika and 2 pieces to Mohan. What fraction of Candy bar is left with him?

3. While calculating perimeter of her garden Ratna calculated the length and breadth of the garden. It was 1500 m long and 600 m wide. _____ times the sum total of length and _________ will be the perimeter of the garden. Find the perimeter in km.

4. For a punch bowl, Carin needs a block of ice with a volume of at least 125 cubic inches. She has a cube of ice that is five inches on each side. Write the volume of the cube using a base and exponents. Then write it in standard form. Is the block

of ice big enough? Remember that volume is calculated by multiplying length times width times height.

5. Tickets to the school play cost Rs 300 for adults and Rs 200 for students. If 235 adults and 322 students attended the play, write an expression that shows the total amount of money made on ticket sales. Then simplify the expression.

6. In 45,657 sum total of place values of 5 = __________

   A: 25   B: 50,500   C: 550   D: 5,050

7. Write greatest fur digit number and smallest five digit number without repeating any oof the digits.

8. There are three cylindrical containers.

   Container II holds 10 times more water than that of I. Container II is three times

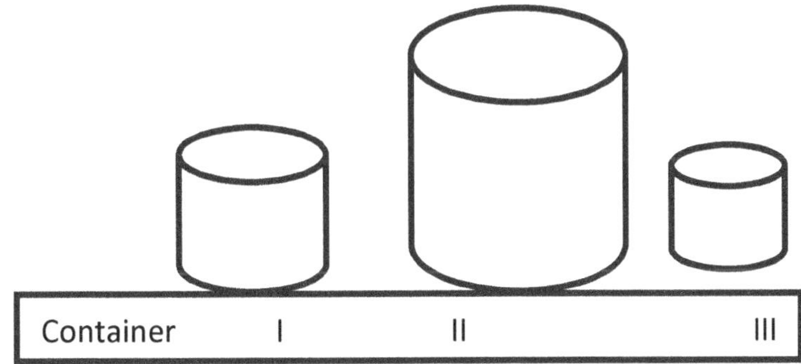

bigger in volume than that of III.

If we use the smallest container for filling up both I and II, then we have to use it for ____times.

A: 30 B: 33 C: 36 D: 48

9. During vacation you spent Rs 127 out of Rs 250. There was another 500 rupees note with you. Find the money left with you.

10. How many seven digit numbers are there in all?

11. $3/19^{th}$ of 38,57,095 = ...

12. What fraction of all the numbers from 1 to 50 are prime numbers?

13. Smallest five digit number divisible by 9 is equal to ....

14. Shapes below shows a definite pattern:

$$\triangle \quad \square \quad \pentagon \quad ....$$

Statements:

I. These are polygons in their increasing order of number of sides.

II. Tenth figure of this pattern will have 12 sides.

III. Fourth figure will be a hexagon.

Which of the above statements are not true?

A: Only a B: Only b C: none D: all

15. What least number must be subtracted from 129 to make it a multiple of 11?

A: 7 B: 8 C: 9 D: 10

16. _________ is obtained if we divide 121.121 by 11.

17. If we add the number 5 to its reciprocal then the value will become _________ (in decimal form).

18. Reflex angle of 39^0 = _________ more than a straight angle.

19. Find the smallest three digit number which can be added to the seven digit smallest number to make the number divisible by 9.

20. 6th multiple of 1,000 is added to the successor of the five digit greatest number. Find the value.

    A: 106,000   B: 600,000   C: 160,000   D: 602,000

21. 7th multiple of 8,000 and 8th multiple of 7,000 added to obtain a value which is _________ more than the smallest 6 digit number.

    A: 36,000   B: 80,000   C: 12,000   D: 16,000

22. Dallas' Renaissance Tower is 1286 feet, Bank of America Complex is 1921 feet, and Bank Two Center is 1787 feet. List the buildings from shortest to tallest.

23. The Timothis are buying a racing car for $63096. They plan to pay in four equal instalments. How much will their each instalments be?

24. After going on vacation, you come home with $5. You spent $11 on a pair of sunglasses, $20.8 on snacks, $401 on purchasing book, and $105.08 on travels. How much money did you start with?

25. Rumila has Rs 10 and Rs 5 coins. Number of Rs 10 coins is two times than number of Rs 5 coins. She has total number of coins equal to 1 less than a hundred. Calculate total amount that she has in her collection.

Worksheet 8

1. Roderick took a car for reaching his office in time. The car was moving with an average speed. It took 4 hours to reach his office which is 240 km away from his house. The car was moving through the second lane of express way having a speed limit of 60 km/h. The speed limit of first lane of that express way is 80 km/h. find the total time which could be saved by Roderick if he prefers moving through the first lane instead of the second.

2. 20 % of a number is 8 more than the 8th multiple of 100. Find the original number.

3. Find the value:

$$\frac{11}{100} + \frac{11}{1000} + \frac{11}{10000} + 0.101 + 1.01 =$$

4. What least number must be subtracted from 121019.049 to make this value exactly divisible by 8 without extending the place of decimals beyond hundredths?

5. The average of six person's age is 12 years. After joining a senior person the average is increased by 3 years 2 months. Find age of the senior.

6. A number is increased by 6.6 to make it a five digit smallest natural number exactly divisible by 11. Find the original number.

7. Donadoni is 4 years older than Mike, who is again 3.5 years younger than Rick. Rick will enter his teenage after 3 years. Find the age of all the fellows.

8. Add the following:

   40% of 64 + 25% of 81 + 50% of 125

9. Subtract 14 thousandths from 14 tenths and multiply the result by 5 hundredths.

10. Richardson throws a baseball at a speed of 72 km/h and his counterpart Ambarish throws it at an average speed of 20 m/s. who throws the ball at a greater speed?

11. Add the following fractions:

$$6\frac{2}{11} + 5\frac{3}{33} + 4\frac{5}{55} + 3\frac{1}{22}$$

12. First angle of a scalene triangle is two times of the second angle and half of the third angle. Find all the three angles.

13. Simplify the following: 8 + {22 X [15 + (14 X 2)]}

14. Which decimal is equivalent to the following expression?

$$\frac{101}{1000} \; X \frac{11}{100} \; X \frac{1}{10} \; X \frac{1}{100} \; X \; 3{,}000$$

15. A cistern can fill up an empty tank of water in 45 minutes, while another cistern will take 1 hour 30 minutes to fill up the same tank. Find the time taken by both the tank to fill up the same empty water tank.

16. Solve the following equation :

$$a = \frac{11}{144} X \frac{12}{169} \ X \frac{13}{121} X \frac{132}{341} \ X \frac{682}{1001} \ X \frac{13}{19}$$

17. Pallav paints half of a wall in 4 hours and quarter of another wall in 3 hours. He can finish painting both the wall completely while working 6 hours a day in _____ days.

18. Chintawar observed that sum total of square of two consecutive number is 265. Both the numbers are two digit numbers. Difference of both the square value is 23. Find both the numbers.

19. Comlete the following:

    a. _____ is the smallest prime number of two digits.

    b. A ________________ having no definite length can be extended endlessly in both the directions.

    c. ____________ is a smallest possible polygon having ____ sides and ______ vertices.

    d. 20 less than 12% of 30% of 1000 = ________________.

    e. 20% of a number exceeds smallest three digit number by 20. Find the number.

20.Simlify:

    a) 3,875 × 12   b) 56,049 × 78   c) 29,647 × 392   d) 50,048 × 504

    d) 5,642 ÷ 7   e) 23,579 ÷ 14   f) 46,968 ÷ 38   d) 69,500 ÷ 250

21. Write the missing angle in the following groups representing angles of a triangle.

    a. 32^0 , _______, 78^0 b. 52^0 , _______, 98^0 c. 132^0 , _______, 18^0

22: Is there similarity in between following fractions? What types of fractions are there in the following list?

$$\frac{3}{9}, \frac{9}{27}, \frac{103}{309}, \frac{3009}{9027}, \frac{21063}{63189} ;$$

23: A triangle having more than one ________ angle or more than one ________ angle is not possible.

24: A regular heptagon has _____ lines of symmetry.

25: "This geometrical shape has no definite length. It can be extended endlessly in either direction. It has no end points." Identify the shape.

26: Rita can finish her assignment in 4 days while wrking 5 hours a day. She started working 4 hours a day from the day 1. In how many days does she can finish her assignment? [Rate of functioning remains unchanged.]

27: "A prime number has exactly two factors, 1 and itself. A composite number is a number greater than 1 with more than two factors. 0 and 1 are neither prime nor composite." On the basis of the given statement check if following numbers are composite or prime.

    (a) 129   (b) 97   (c) 1002   (d) 10,008

Worksheet 9

1. How many four digit numbers are there in all?
2. Complementary angle oof 23^0 19' is equal to ……………
3. $1/11^{th}$ of 121,242,066 + $1/13^{th}$ of 169,338,078 = …………………
4. Greatest number of six digits divisible by 8 = …………………
5. Represent data in a table form and answer the questions as follows:

   The Sahara Desert in Africa has an area of 3,500,000 square miles. The Simpson Desert in Australia has an area of 56,000 square miles. In North America, the Mojave Desert has an area of 15,000 square miles; and the Kalahari Desert in Africa has an area of 275,000 square miles.

Name of Deserts	Area (sq. miles)
Sahara (Africa)	
	56,000
	275,000

   I.   Which desert is having maximum area?

  II.   Arrange these deserts in ascending order of their area.

 III.   ___________ and ___________________ deserts are located in the same continent.

 IV.   ________________ is a desert with a least area and by part it is _______ of the greatest one.

> In the same way you can make a chart of 15 major deserts having adequate expansion.

6. Sahana wanted to divide 209, 2009 and 20,009 by a definite divisor and received remainders 2 in each case.

Statements:

I. Specified divisor is a common factor of all the three dividends duly provided.

II. Before working out the divisor we can subtract 2 from all the three dividends and then we try to find out a common divisor for them all.

III. Guessing about such divisor without subtracting the remainder is not possible.

IV. There are more than one common divisors of such type.

Which of the statements are not appropriate?

A: I, III and IV   B: Only IV   C: II and III

7. Three squares of side 30 cm each joined side by side to make a rectangle. Find the outer boundary of that rectangle.

8. What smallest number must be added to a seven digit smallest number to make it a multiple of 33?

9. Rohit covers up 12 km 60 m by running four times around a square sized play ground. Find the side of that square sized play ground.

10. What number of least value must be subtracted from 121.125 to make it divisible by 11?

11. Express 72 as product of its prime factors.

12. Write the following numbers as a product of their prime factors:

    a) 129 =

    b) 121 =

    c) 144 =

13. The average surface temperature on Saturn is 134K. Express this temperature in degrees Celsius.

14. The average surface temperature on the dwarf planet Pluto is 50K. Express this temperature in degrees Celsius.

15. The Sun has several regions. The apparent surface that we can see from a distance is called the photosphere. Temperatures of the photosphere range from 5,000 °C to 8,000 °C. Express this temperature range in Kelvin.

16. The chromosphere is a hot layer of plasma just above the photosphere. Chromosphere temperatures can reach 10,000 °C. Express this temperature in Kelvin.

17. The outermost layer of the Sun's atmosphere is called the corona. Its temperatures can reach over 1,000,000 °C. Express this temperature in Kelvin.

18. Nuclear fusion takes place in the center, or core, of the Sun. Temperatures there can reach 15,000,000 °C. Express this temperature in Kelvin.

19. Surface temperatures on Mercury can reach 660 °F. Express this temperature in Kelvin (K).   ($273^0C = 1K$)

20. Surface temperatures on Venus, the hottest planet in our solar system, can reach 755K. Express this temperature in degrees Fahrenheit.

21. Observe factorisation of 36 and 90.

    36 = 2 X 3 X 3 X 2;   90 = 2 X 3 X 3 X 5;

    Find HCF of 36 and 90. Which statements are true?

  I.   HCF stands for Highest Common Factor (HCF) or Greatest Common Divisor.

  II.   HCF of a group of numbers divides those numbers individually without leaving remainders.

III.   HCF can be obtained by multiplying common factors of constituent numbers of the group.

IV.   All common factors of numbers are not included in the HCF.

A: Only I , II and III B: Only II and IV   C: Only IV   D: None of the above.

22. In the calculation table depicted below numbers are related to each other. Find their inter relations and also identify missing numbers.

d	1000	c
a	b	81
6,036	6000	36

Options

	a	b	c	d
A:	1001	9000	1	1001
B:	9081	9000	9	1009
C:	2018	4000	27	3009
D:	9000	7000	36	9081

23. 121 has _________ factors.

Statement : 1221 is a composite numbers.

Reason   : 1221 has more than two factors.

A: The given reason is appropriate.

B: The given reason is not correct.

C: The given reason requires more explanation.

D: Both the statement and reason are wrong.

24. Observe following statements:

I: 97 is an odd prime number.

II: 97 has no factors other than 1 and the number itself.

III: 97 has another factor which is also a factor of all the other natural numbers.

IV: All the other odd numbers are multiples of 97.

Select which of the statements mentioned above are true.

A: Only I   B: Only II   C: Only I , II and III   D: All

25. Some of the properties of prime and composite numbers are given below.

I : 1 is not a prime *or* composite number.

II : Two is the only even prime number.

III: All odd numbers are not prime.

IV: All composite numbers can be written as product of prime numbers.

V: 101 has only two factors 1 and the number itself. That is why it is a prime number

VI : We cannot consider 1 as one of the factor of any prime number.

Which of the above statements are not true?

A: Only I   B: Only VI

C: I, II , III and IV   D: Only II, III and IV

26. A greatest possible 3 digit number that divides 278.139 exactly without leaving any remainder is ___________ .

27. If we continue the following pattern:

5,000,   4,250,   3,500 ,   2,750 ,   a , b , c.

$b \div (a \times c) = d;$ and $b \div a \times c = e$

Expand d : ______ $= \dfrac{}{10} + \dfrac{}{100} + \dfrac{}{1000} + \dfrac{}{10000}$

Options:

   I.   d is a decimal number .

   II.   The value of d has four place decimal. It can be expanded up to ten thousandths place.

   III.   Values of d and e are different.

   IV.   Value of e is closure to that of d.

Which of the statements are not true?

A: I, III and IV   B: II and IV

C: Only IV   D: None

28. Sum total of the smallest and the greatest four digit numbers formed by using 4,7,9 and 0 without repeating any digits twice is ___G____ more than the smallest five digit number.

9,740 + 4,079 = G. Here G stands for ________

A: 763   B: 819   C: 989   D: 1209

29. There are ___ more lines of symmetry in figure H than in figure I.

H

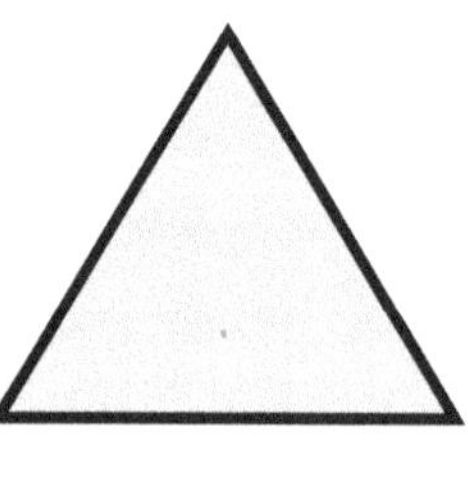

I

Statement   : Regular polygons exhibit symmetry.

Reason   : Sides and angles are equal to each other.

Select Option(s)..

  I.   Reason satisfies the statement and makes it true.

  II.   Reason given is not adequate for drawing any conclusion.

  III.   There exists mismatch between Statement and reason.

  IV.   Lines of symmetry has no relationship with the nature of a polygon.

30. At 3 O Clock and 9 O Click both hour hand and minute hand of a clock makes an angle of ___a_____ which is __b__ of a complete angle.

A: a= 90^0 b = $1/4^{th}$ B: a= 180^0 b = $1/2^{nd}$

C: a= 270^0 b = $1/3^{rd}$ D: a= 30^0 b = $1/12^{th}$

Worksheet 11

1. Simplify $5 + (8 \times 2) + (5 \times 3)$

2. Observe the following patterns:

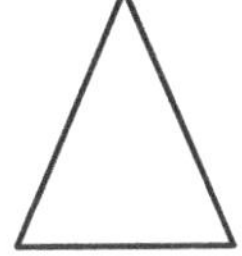 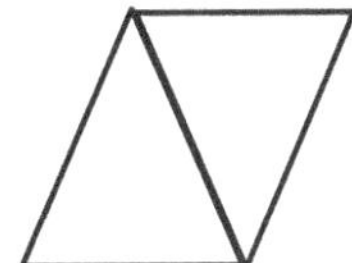 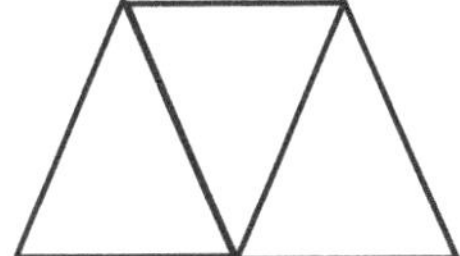 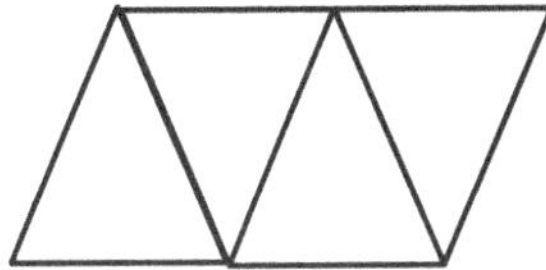

   a) Count the number of line segments in each shape.

   b) How many line segments will 9 such shapes contain?

   c) Write the rule for the above pattern.

3. $1 + 3 = 2^2$; $1 + 3 + 5 = 3^2$; $1 + 3 + 5 + 7 = 4^2$; Similarly

a) $1 + 3 + ... + 51 =$ _______;   b) Sum of first 100 consecutive odd numbers = _______;

c) $(1 + 3 + 5 + ... + 19) - 100 =$ _______;   d) Sum of first 20 odd numbers $- 300 =$ _______;

4. The greatest 4 digit multiple of 8 + smallest four digit multiple of 3 = _______.

5. 2% of 3% of 4% of 1001 = _______;

6. Half of a quarter of 16016 + one third of five sixth of 18018 = _______.

7. All the English alphabets are replaced by numbers from 1 to 26. In this way 1 stands for A, 3 for C and so on.

   Decode the given message on the basis of above code.

       9   12   15   22   5   13   25   9   14   4   9   1

    _______   _______   _______   _______

8. What least number must be added to 101,090,809 to make the number a multiple of 4?

9. A vessel contains 5l 400 ml of milk. For how many people can this milk be distributed so that each gets 40 ml ?

10. A biscuit factory produces 6,120 pack of biscuits in a day. How many packs of biscuits are produced in 6 days at the same rate ? These packs are sealed in boxes by filling 20 packs in each box. How many boxes are required to fill all these packs of biscuits produced in 6 days?

11. A drum contains 68 l 750 ml of honey. This is again filled in 5 cans equally. What is the quantity of honey in each can ? Honey of one of these cans is to be filled in bottles so that each bottle contains 250 ml. Then how many bottles are required to fill the honey ?

12. What fraction of all the numbers from 1 to 100 are multiples of 9?

13. How many times do 7 occur if we write all the natural numbers from 1 to 100?

14. Estimate the numbers to the highest place and find the total estimated result.

  a) 1) 5680 + 3250 + 850 2) 67,430 + 24,549 + 19,590

  b) 1) 48,350 − 39,520 2) 42,990 − 29,005

  c) 1) 348 × 27 2) 590 × 42 3) 5,870 × 34 4) 6,720 × 132

  d) 1) 279 ÷ 18 2) 342 ÷ 33 3) 8,459 ÷ 39 4) 12,520 ÷ 98

15. Complete the following:

 a) Fractions _________be shown on a number line. Every fraction has a _______ associated with it on the number line.

 b) In a _________ fraction, the numerator is less than the denominator. The fractions, where the

  numerator is _________ than the denominator are called improper fractions.

c) An ______________ fraction can be written as a combination of a whole and a part.

d) Fraction combined with whole number and a part of whole is called __________ fractions.

e) Each proper or improper fraction has many ______________ fractions.

f) To find any ________________ fraction of a given fraction, we may multiply or divide both the numerator and the denominator of the given fraction by the same number.

g) Any two decimal numbers can be compared among themselves. The comparison can start with the __________ part. If such parts are equal then the tenth part can be compared and so on.

h) ______________ are used in many ways in our lives. For example, in representing units of money, length and weight.

i) All numbers can be exressed in their ______________ forms. We can express 3 as 3.0000.

j) 1.32, 2.43, 1.01, 0.06 and 1,08 are ______________ decimals as they have same numbers of decimal places.

k) ______________ having denominator 100 or having two places of values less than 1 is called a percentage.

16. If six cubes of dimensions 2 cm by 2cm by 2cm are placed side by side, what would the dimensions of the resulting cuboid be?

17. Some fifth graders experimented with the growth of plants in different types of soil. They recorded the results in a table. What was the total amount of plant growth over the two-week period for each type of soil?

18. Some fifth graders experimented with the growth of plants in different types of soil. They recorded the results in a table. What was the total amount of plant growth over the two-week period for each type of soil?

19. Which greatest six digit number is a common multiple of 2, 4, 8 and 16?

20. Monikornika planted salings at a uniform interval of 2 m beside the longer side of the lawn beside her house. Length of the lawn is 96 m. Only the outer side is used for plantation works. Find the number of saplings used for this work.

21. 11 X 11 = 121; 111 X 111 = 12321; Now find the following: ---

a) 11 X 125 X 11 X 8 = ___________;   b) 111 X 40 X 111 X 25 = _____________;

c) 1111 X 1111 = _____________;   d) 11111 X 11111 = _____________;

22. How many symmetry lines are there in a regular pentagon?

23. $\left(1 + \frac{1}{10}\right)\left(1 + \frac{1}{11}\right) .. \left(1 + \frac{1}{1000}\right) X \frac{101}{1001} =$ _____________.

24: The floor of a room a hotel is 12 m long and 10 m wide. 45 tiles of 1 m square was in stock. Tiles come in market in pack of ten tiles. How many more 1m square tiles does the manager need to completely cover the floors of three such rooms?

      I: 15 tiles more than 30 full pack   II: 5 tiles more than 31 full pack

      III: 25 tiles more than 29 full pack   IV: 50 tiles more than 25 full pack

      Select your answers

      A: Only I   B: Only II   C: I, II and III   D: Only IV

25: How many five digit even numbers are there in all?

26: Temperature of a city increased from 23^0 C to a highere scale of 42^0 C. There is an increase of 1.8^0 F for every corresponding increase of 1^0 C. Calculate corresponding increase of temperature of that city in ^{0} F.

27: $11/19^{th}$ of $19/39^{th}$ of 39,78,078 = ...

Worksheet 12

1. If $\dfrac{2}{5}$ of $40 = \dfrac{2}{5} \times 40 = \dfrac{2 \times 40}{5} = 2 \times 8 = 16$

   a. What is $\dfrac{3}{5}$ of 60 ?

2. Add : $\dfrac{2}{10} + \dfrac{33}{100} + \dfrac{121}{1000} + \dfrac{6}{5}$

3. 19 + 19 tenths + 19 thousandths = ____________.

4. $3\dfrac{1}{2} + 11\dfrac{7}{8} =$

5. Half of a quarter of 64 = ____________________.

6. Multiply : $\dfrac{10}{121} \times \dfrac{11}{100} \times \dfrac{13}{24} \times \dfrac{11}{26} \times \dfrac{4}{5} =$

7. Tap A can fill up a water tank in 30 minutes and tap B can empty the same water tank in 45 minutes. Tap A will take _____ minutes to fill the tank when both the taps remain open.

8. A cistern can fill a water tank in 45 minutes and a tap can empty the same water tank in 1 hour 30 minutes. Find the time taken up by the cistern to fill the tank when the tap kept open.

9. Three triangles joined side by side to form a polygon having ___ sides. Sum total of all the interior angles of this polygon is _____^{0}.

   [Angle Sum Property of a Triangle: Sum total of all the interior angles of a triangle is 180^0.]

10. Half of a number exceeds 2009 by 108. Find out the number.

11. Quarter of a number is two times bigger than smallest five digit number. Find out $1/10^{th}$ of that number.

12. After turning three times by making right angles at the centre Sonalika was facing North direction. What was the initial direction that she was facing?

13. Fill in the blanks:

    a. Exterior angles of a polygon are 1st , 2nd 3rd and 4th multiple of 36^0. Find all the interior angles of this polygon.

    [Exterior angle along with corresponding interior angle of any polygon are supplementary to each other.]

    b. Interior angles of a triangle are first second and third multiples of 30^0. Find the angles. What is the special name of that triangle?

    c. A triangle having _________ right angles is not possible.

    d. A triangle having _______ obtuse angles is not possible.

    e. Sum total of all the interior angles of a polygon is 540^0. Find the number of sides it has. There are ______ diagonals in this polygon.

    f. Sum total of all the interior angles of a polygon is equal to four right angles. It must have at least one ______ angle or at least _______ right angles. They cannot have less than ______ obtuse angles.

    g. Identify following triangles:

    h. Supplementary angle of complementary angle of 56^0 is equal to

    ____________________.

    i. A quadrilateral having maximum number of ______ right angles is possible.

    j. What fraction of right angle is 30^0?

    k. A quadrilateral having maximum number of _____ acute angles is possible.

    l. A triangle having two _______ angles or two _______ angles is not possible.

Worksheet 13

1: Following data chart shows population of birds in a city zoo.

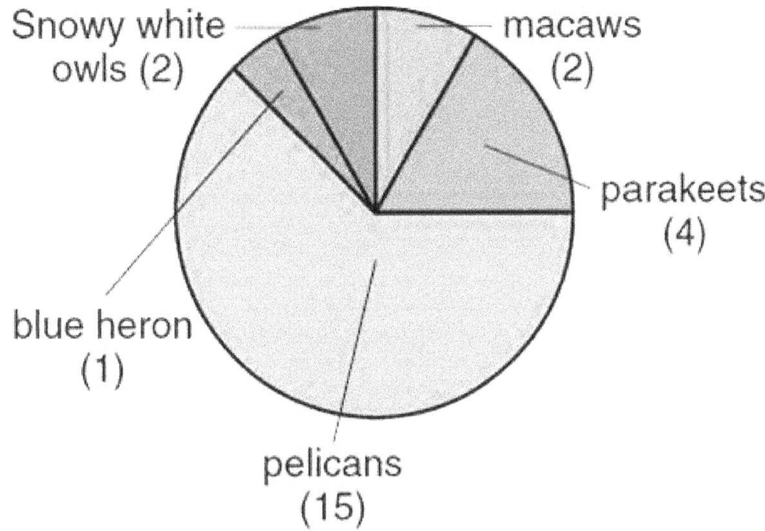

Q a. Population of which bird is recorded maximum?

Q b. What fraction of the population is occupied by macraw and parakeets?

Q c. Population of which bird is recorded minimum and by what fraction?

Q what fraction of birds in the zoo are blue herons?

2: Snehal and Rita works together to finish a work in 12 days, Rita and Anita can finish it in 14 days; Anita and Snehal can finish the same in 13 days. All the three fellow friends started working together to finish the same work together in …….. days.

3. If $\dfrac{11A}{13} = \dfrac{12B}{17} = \dfrac{13C}{19}$; $then$ $\dfrac{(A+B)(B+C)(C+A)}{3ABC} = \cdots \ldots$

4. What fraction of sum of one ninth of four digit greatest number and half of smallest five digit number is equal to 179?

5. What fraction of all the natural numbers starting from 1 to 5000 are common multiples of 5 and 25?

6. Is there any pair of natural number having LCM 1009 and HCF 169?

7. $(0.0121 \times 0.002 \times 0.05 \times 0.02) \times 10^5 = \ldots\ldots\ldots\ldots$

8. What digit should be there at tenths place if we multiply 1.25, 0.4, 2,5 and 0.08? Write each of the following decimals.

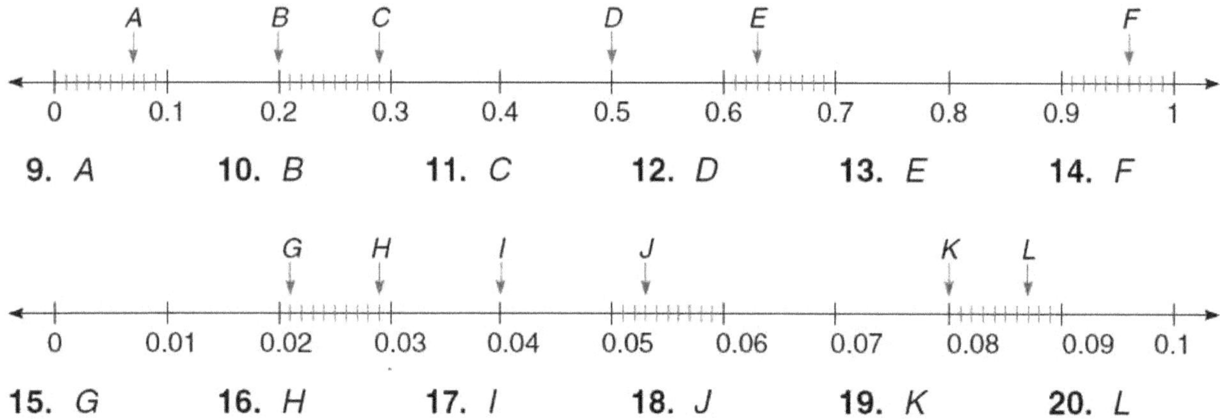

9. *A*   **10.** *B*   **11.** *C*   **12.** *D*   **13.** *E*   **14.** *F*

15. *G*   **16.** *H*   **17.** *I*   **18.** *J*   **19.** *K*   **20.** *L*

21. Sum of a natural and its reciprocal is equal to 4.25. Find out the sixth multiple of that number.

22. Three interior angles of a triangle are in the ratio of 3: 5: 8. Find out magnitude of the greatest angle of that triangle.

23. Volume of a cubical block is equal to 1331 sq. cm. Six such blocks are arranged side by side to form a cuboid. Find out length of that cuboid.

24. Elaine rode her bike 4.93 mi on Thursday, 3.45 mi on Friday, 5.38 mi on Saturday, and 6.35 mi on Sunday. About how many miles did she ride her bike in these three days?

25. What least number should be subtracted from seven digit greatest number to obtain a common multiple of 4, 8, 12 and 16?

26. $0.583 + 2.745$ $\ldots\ldots\ldots\ldots$ $0.1 + 0.02 + 3.003$

27. $0.001 + 1.001 + 11.011 + 101.101 - 121 = \ldots\ldots\ldots\ldots$

Worksheet 14

1. Complete the following number pattern:

a) 88,_______, __________, __________, 33, __________. __________.

b) 121, _________, __________, _________, _______, 55, _____, _________, 22, 11

c) 12, ____, ________, 12,345, ______________.

d) 10204, ______, ___________, _______________, ___________ , 12,204, 12,404.

e) 144, ______, ___________, _______________, 96, 84 , _________, _______.

2. Add : MMDCXX + MCDXCLVI

3. Subtract: MMMCLX – MCMLXXXV

4. Arrange the following in ascending and descending order:

a) MDC, MCMLXV, MCDXCLV, MDLXVIII

b) XXII, XXXVIII, XCLXXVI, XVI

c) MMMCMXCIX, MMMXII, MMMCMXXII,

5. Compare:

a) MMMCMXCIX ______ MMMDCXCIX;

b) CMCCX _________ MCCX

c) XXIV _______XXXIII

6. Complete the following:

36,653   = ______   + ___ + ____ +___ + ________.

7. 2,892   =   X 1000 + …. X 100   + …. X 10   + ……..X 1

8. Complete the following:

a) ______________ are what we can multiply to get numbers.

b) ______________ are what we get after multiplying the number by any other

number.

c) ______________ is a factor of all the numbers.

d) All the numbers are one of the multiple of ______________.

e) All ______________ numbers have only two factors, 1 and the number itself.

f) 36 has ______________ factors in all.

g) 36 has ______________ prime factors in all.

h) All the factors of 18 are also ______________ of 36, but all the ______________ of 36 are not the factors of 18.

i) ______________ are always greater than or equal to the number.

9. Multiples of 4 are also multiples of 2, but all multiples of 2 are not necessarily multiples of ______________.

10. ______________ is the smallest three digit number divisible by 8.

11. ____ must be added to the three digit smallest number to make it exactly divisible by 9 .

12. The greatest possible five digit number formed by different digits without repeating any of the digits twice.

13. Area of each white tiles in the pattern is 25 cm^2. white tiles are arranged in a uniform sequential pattern. Length of this shape is ________ cm, its breadth is ______ cm and area is ____________ square cm.

14. 27 tenths + 43 hundredths + 13 tens = ______________.

15. If 10% of 5% of 48 = $\dfrac{48}{50} = \dfrac{48X2}{50X2} = \dfrac{96}{100} = 0.96$, then calculate the value of 4% of 5% of 109.

16. A 6 digit greatest number which is obtained by using 6,4,7,0, 2 and 9 without repeating them = ______________.

17. What least number must be subtracted from 179 to make it a multiple of 13?

Worksheet 15

1. Dana has only 2 rupees coins in her hand, and Ajah has exactly the same number of 5 rupees coins and no other coins. Together they have a total of Rs. 210. How many coins is each person holding? Find their individual shares in the collection.

2. When 2 pieces of rope are placed end-to-end, they measure 40 meters in length. When the 2 pieces are laid side-by-side, one is 10 meters longer than the other. How long is each piece of rope? Show your work.

3. Observe the figure and answer the following:

   a) How many cubical boxes are there?

   b) How many more boxes are needed to make it a complete cuboidal block?

   c) If volume of 1 box is 10 cm^2 , then find the volume of all boxes.

4. If 1 is added to a number it becomes a third multiple of 900900. Find the number.

5. Find the greatest and smallest 4 digit number without repeating any digits. Also find their difference.

6. A circle of diameter 14 cm is exactly fitted concentrically inside another circle of diameter 28 cm for obtaining a design find the area enclosed by linings of both the circle.

7. What must be added to 12109 to make it a complete square number?

8. ______ is the sixteenth multiple of the smallest composite number of a digit.

9. Half of 20% of 1600 = __________

10. 9th multiple of 9 is ______ more than 7th multiple of 7.

11. Calculate the fraction of "M" present in the word "Mathematics."

12. Mandela wanted to find out a number which is a sum of square values of three consecutive even numbers. The sum total was 308. Find all the three numbers.

13. What least number must be subtracted from 1332 to make it a multiple of 11?

14. Half of 4/9th of 810 = ______________

15. Mohan scored full marks in Mathematics. Dinesh got 6 less than Mohan in Mathematics. His score was 12 more than Latika. Full Marks in Mathematics was 100. Find the score of Latika.

16. ______ Dozens is just half of a gross.

17. Average age of 12 students was 12.8 years. After a new admission in their group the average age of the group became 13 years. Find the age of newly admitted fellow.

18. Sum total of place values of 5 in the following numbers = ______

      15,647;   51,780;   12,505

19. Day before yesterday was Sunday. Day after tomorrow will be __

20. The greatest possible 5 digit number divisible by 4 is ______ less than the smallest 6 digit number.

21. Monika added 3210 to number for obtaining the greatest even number of four digits. Find the number.

22. What least number must be subtracted from a five digit smallest odd number to make it a multiple of 11?

23. How many three digit numbers can be formed by using digits 3,5 and 0? Arrange these numbers in ascending order.

24. What fraction of 100 is equal to ten times of 36 tenths?

25. Rita used half of the colours she had in stock. There were only 7 out of 12 poster colours in her stock. After using half of it what fraction of her stock left with her?

26. Certain number becomes a three digit greatest even number after subtracting ________ from the smallest four digit number.

27. A polygon is ____________ if any part of a diagonal contains points in the exterior of the polygon. If no diagonal contains points in the exterior, then the polygon is ______.

28. Observe the place value chart carefully

Thousands	Hundreds	Tens	Ones	Decimal point	Tenths	Hundredths	thousandths		
7		5	2	.	4	8			
	1	3	8		0	0	9		
	3	0	7		1	3	9		
1					4	3			
	3	4	8		9	8	7		
7	8	5	2	.	7	9	2		

29. Kim gathered information about the population of individual states of her country. If she prepares a bar graph of this data, what information will be displayed on the vertical axis? What information will be displayed on the horizontal axis?

30. Total cost of 3 snacks and two breads is Rs. 11. In other combination total cost of 2 snacks and 3 breads is Rs. 9. What will be the total cost of a snacks and a bread?

31. What least number must be multiplied to 72 to make the value a perfect square?

32. Express the following decimal in mixed number:

    a. 800.03 = _______ 3/100;

    b. 29.029 = _______

    c. 8.019 + 2.881 + 3.008 = ___________ .

33. $\frac{11}{23}$ of $\frac{23}{48}$ of $\frac{48}{97}$ of 194 = _____ .

34: Two sets of pillars counted by a visitor from standing in the middle. He has counted number of pillars from right hand side along with the pillar that he was holding as 10. From left hand side his counting in the same way was 9. How many pillars were there? Consider the fact that none of the pillars were identical.

35: Monika calculated 15th multiple of 5 added to 5th multiple of 15. Find the digit that she might have in the one's place of the product.

36: There are ________ flat faces and ____ curved faces in a cuboid.

37: Find the difference of place values of 5 in 22,543 and 54,432.

38: Renuka prepared a bar graph that shows the number of kg of food eaten each day by each animal. What information goes on the horizontal axis? What information can be placed on the vertical axis?

39: (4 ten thousands 2 thousands) X 100 = ...

40: 32 tens + 29 hundreds + 102 thousands = ...

41: How many three digit numbers can be made by using digits 3, 5 and 8 only once in each case? Arrange all such numbers in ascending order.

42: 2/3rd of 3/7th of a natural number is equal to 40,80,012. Find out the number.

43: What least number should be subtracted from three digit greatest number to obtain a common multiple of 3 and 6?